OVERCOMING
Emotional Baggage

A Woman's Guide To
Living The Abundant Life

Gladys Famoriyo

Overcoming Emotional Baggage: A Woman's Guide to Living the Abundant Life

ISBN 0-924748-73-7
UPC 88571300043-7

Printed in the United States of America
© 2006 by Gladys Famoriyo

Cover Photo by DNC Photography LTD
Makeup by Sarah Famoriyo.

Milestones International Publishers
140 Danika Drive NW
Huntsville, AL 35806
Phone: 256.830.0362; Fax: 256.830.9206
www.milestonesintl.com

Please note that *Overcoming Emotional Baggage* has been written and designed to conform to British standards of usage.

1 2 3 4 5 6 7 8 9 10 11 / 09 08 07 06

Dedication

This book is dedicated to my mother, Mrs. Joyce Famoriyo – a woman who stands out among other women. I believe my passion to touch people's lives emanated from this great woman whose whole existence is the epitome of walking with the Holy Spirit. Thank you for standing with me, believing in me, encouraging me, sacrificing for me and constantly praying for me. You are a role model to me. You inspire me in more ways than words can say. Your light will continually shine even after you have left us and your works will be remembered. I believe I speak for both your biological and spiritual children by saying that there are many virtuous women in the world, but you surpass them all. May you live long enough to enjoy the fruits of your labours.

Acknowledgments

I thank You, Father God, for giving me air in my lungs and for considering me as a worthy vessel to do Your work. For this, I will remain indebted to You for eternity, because I certainly don't deserve it. Thanks for making me the apple of Your eyes. What more could any princess ask for? Moreover, where would I be without You?

Special thanks to my dad, Mr. J.A. Famoriyo. As for the darlings God gave me in the form of sisters — Deborah, Sarah, and Elizabeth; I appreciate the fact that through your own individual uniqueness, you have brought immense joy into my life – much more than you will ever know. Thanks for your patience and support as I strove to do all the things God lay on my heart. Sam, my "big bruv" – I love you. I have always maintained that God gave me the best ever siblings, and I will always cherish you all.

I would like to extend special thanks to all those who made this dream a reality. To Jim Rill, my publisher, and his team for being so accommodating towards me. Thanks to Donna Beech, my editor, for helping me say exactly what I meant to say. Please accept miles of smiles and bunches of hugs from me to you.

Finally, to all my friends, colleagues, mentors, coaches and pastors who have sown seeds of encouragement, wisdom and expertise in my life over the years. You know who you are. I thank you from the bottom of my heart. I pray God rewards you immensely.

Contents

CONTENTS

Introduction

*Y*ou might be thinking, *"Oh no, not another book about dealing with emotions"*. I thought so myself when I first felt inspired to write it. However, that's why I was determined to make this one different. Instead of writing another predictable book about emotions, I wanted to create one that would really make you stop and think. Its primary aim is to support you in living the authentic, fulfilled, prosperous and purposeful life God ordained for you to live. So, Sister, please don't put this book down unless you can say, hand-on-your-heart, that you have your emotional life in order and you are where God wants you to be in every facet of your life. Even if you have gotten things in order, I hope you will find this book refreshing with some powerful insights and new nuggets to digest. Whatever path you are travelling along in life, this book will support you in overcoming any emotional baggage you may be harboring (known and unknown to you) and help you start to live a more meaningful life, filled with true fulfilment, joy and purpose.

Brace yourself for an incredible, life-changing journey!

ॐ

Since childhood, I have always been one who strove to be the best "me" ever. From a tender age, I was extremely optimistic and motivated by the fact that the sky was not the limit and that I could soar beyond the skies if I wanted to. In my world, anything was possible. This is a belief I still hold onto fervently.

As you may appreciate, life as a youngster is not usually as complicated as life as an adult. So childhood gave me the opportunity to focus on excelling in two specific areas: spirituality and academics. Developing my spirituality consisted of building my relationship with God by reading my kiddies' book of Bible stories, praying, going to Church, dreaming of what Heaven would be like and striving to make sure that I made it there. As for my academics, I soared both in my normal school and Sunday school, as I gulped down all there was to know. Along the way, I won quite a few competitions and awards.

You might be wondering how I became extremely optimistic and believed the impossible could exist at such an early age. Well, I'll share a secret with you. It did not happen overnight. I wouldn't say I was born that way. However, my beliefs, attitudes and behaviors were ultimately fuelled by rummaging through my very first full version Bible given to me around the age of 7 or 8, digesting its contents and setting high standards for my life based on the stories, principles, promises and truths I gleaned from it.

As far as I was concerned (and still am), if it is in the Bible, it is there for me to partake of. When God said, *"Nothing is impossible to those who believe,"* I believed it. When He said, *"I can do all things through Christ Jesus,"* I believed that too. When He said, *"Faith without works* [i.e., action] *is dead,"* I coupled action with my faith. And the list goes on.

I guess you can say it all started when I believed and digested some big truths and principles until they became a part of me. As a child, I found it a simple process, but little did I know that what I was actually doing by fully embracing God's Word was taking steps to living a fulfilled, prosperous and purposeful life – which God promised us all.

One of the biblical truths I ingested was the fact that Jesus Christ came to give us life – an abundant life (John 10:10). Therefore, as far as I was concerned – being the perpetual optimist and big thinker — this principle was meant to encompass every facet of my life — every nook and cranny of my tripartite being (spirit, soul and body). So as I grew up, I endeavored to ensure that an abundant life became a reality for me.

Some years later, I blossomed into a young lady. Still holding on to my biblical truths, promises and principles, I continued to excel in my spirituality. My focus on my academic life soon switched to my professional life.

Believing *anything was possible* meant that the notion of something being impossible to achieve or that anything could separate me from God's plan for my life simply did not exist. No matter what happened, I held on to God's Word. After all, He is almighty God to whom all power belongs.

This mindset helped me a great deal. Determination, perseverance and enthusiasm also became good friends of mine in the early days of my journey in life. I must admit that hanging out with these friends paid off – especially in those times when my reality couldn't have been any further from my desires. And so this was how life was for me.

I'm sure you've experienced a similar thing. As we make our way through our formative years, we go through life experiences and circumstances that complicate our lives. Some good. Some bad. And some downright ugly. Sometimes we may pick up and internalise some beliefs, attitudes and behaviours that don't benefit us. It may be a coping behavior to help us deal with the things we go through. We may even compensate for not getting our personal needs met, even if we do it in the wrong way. So as we make our way through life, we accumulate all this stuff. Consciously or not, a number of us bury these things deep within our souls. Doing this is detrimental. It has the potential to impact us in a negative way, especially if we do not deal with it in an appropriate manner. We'll talk more later in the book about the ways in which it can sear, destroy, hinder and sabotage the very life we seek.

Remember I said that I believed Jesus Christ came to give us the abundant life and this was to span into every facet of our lives? I did say *"every facet of our lives,"* didn't I? This means *every* part of our being and all that concerns us. That's the good news – we were not meant to be hindered and blocked. We were meant to thrive.

When I took my place in the rat race of life — joining the hordes of other go-getters — I adopted a popular approach to dealing with one's emotional baggage. In order to cope with it all, I left one important part of my tripartite being behind: my soul, i.e., my mind, will and emotions.

The rat race focused on external things such as success, amassing personal wealth that afforded a particular kind of lifestyle, being *super skinny*, fitting into social cliques, wearing the right clothes, eating in trendy restaurants, travelling to exotic locations and having fun in life. These things (with a few exceptions) were not bad in themselves. But when they started to rule our lives and became our reason for living, that's when we appear to have totally lost the plot!

For the spiritual among us go-getters, spirituality meant anything from having a deep and meaningful relationship with God to falling for the latest fad, religion or guru that popped its head into our ultra *"I-want-to-fit-in,"* pleasure-seeking society. As for our souls, they were simply left out of the loop. After all, we were too busy chasing things.

To make matters worse, no one ever seemed to talk about the soul — much less do anything about it. The idea of focusing on one's "soul" was actually considered *"fluffy"*, *"touchy-feely"* stuff or even *"non-essential"* to some people. Could you imagine approaching your boss to pay for you to attend a training course aimed at developing and nurturing your soul to improve your personal effectiveness and performance in the workplace? Though your boss might be swayed by words like "improving personal effectiveness and performance", the bottom line is the word "soul" might just put him/her off.

Instead, we focused on other aspects of our lives – leaving behind the care, nurture and development of this integral part of ourselves. I am not sure why this happened, but a number of factors come to mind, such as an unhealthy awareness of one's self, denial, ignorance, disregard for the emotional symptoms we displayed or lack of understanding about how to deal with our emotional life.

Another possible reason was the fact that we were too busy sprinting through life, not slowing down and/or being still enough to catch up with our selves. I discovered that some of us used our *sprinting* technique to evade dealing with our emotional issues. So little or no emphasis was placed on nurturing our souls.

When a perturbing situation arose, instead of dealing with it, a number of us simply added it to the other *stuff* we were already carrying around with us. It was so much easier to brush it underneath a rug – hoping no one would see the baggage we were amassing. After all, this was the trendy thing to do.

And woe betide you, Sister, if people were to find out about your emotional issues — it might just change their perception of you! The last thing a *super-spiritual highflying Sister* needed was people thinking she was weak, incapable or a failure – not being able to handle her own business. (This was true when I got on the fast-lane treadmill and it's just as true to this day. If you don't believe me, try spending some time watching TV. Haven't we made a multi-billion entertainment industry by focusing on other people's negative life experiences and/or inabilities to handle correctly the content of their souls?)

After my own personal experience getting caught on the tread-mills of life, I looked around and sadly realized that a huge number of us — Christian and not — have "matured" into what I call *lopsided adults*. By this I mean that while we have developed certain parts of our being, other parts have been left behind (probably since child-hood). The problem is so endemic in our culture that it's one of the reasons that motivated me to write this book.

A simple analogy for the problem is as follows: Imagine a healthy adult with the reading, writing and mathematical capability of a 7-year-old. Let's say she does not have a learning disability and the reason for her inability to read better is that she skipped classes throughout school and simply never caught up with her peers. And so, here she is 20 or so years later, finding difficulty securing employ-ment. It's something she never learned as she was growing up and it's causing her problems in the present.

In the same way, many adults are walking around with undevel-oped and/or degenerate spirits and souls for varying reasons. However, the good news is that, just as an adult with reading, writ-ing and mathematical difficulties can take classes to improve these skills so that she can function well in society, we can address the undeveloped aspects of our spirits and souls so that we can also oper-ate effectively in our world. It all depends on whether we are willing to invest in ourselves.

Just like our physical body, all facets of our being need nourish-ment, care, rest and development. It is not enough to be soaring in one's career, running a successful business, being financially inde-pendent, having an award-winning body, or even being super-spiri-tual. I don't believe our portion in life is to find ourselves in an either/or situation. God created us to be balanced beings. He wants His daughters to prosper in every facet of their lives. This includes having a healthy emotional life too (3 John 2). So, it's not just a case of having one or the other, but of having all that the Father has stored up for us.

Do you realise that God can actually handle providing you with all these things at the same time? At times, thinking as mere mortals, we feel we cannot handle all these things at once; but God can help us to be effective managers of all the members of our beings.

In this day and time, when we are constantly on the go with our to-do lists growing at phenomenal rates and not having enough time in the day to get everything done, we are compelled to look after our emotional well-being. Better still, we must look out for any negative emotions, symptoms or excess baggage that are indicative of all not being well.

Have you noticed that a lot of our battles take place within our souls, i.e., our minds, wills and emotions? We all experience new challenges on a day-to-day basis — not to mention the conflicts we are still carrying around with us from the past.

If we neglect to take care of our souls, which are so vulnerable, it can hinder us from living the purposeful life God has ordained. Failing to do this may even become a barrier to our accomplishing those things we ardently seek – such as finding fulfilment, joy, a successful career and/or business, marrying a good man, living in marital bliss, raising godly children, accomplishing a lifelong goal or living a meaningful life.

As I mentioned before, as far back as I can remember one of my ultimate goals in life has been to live the abundant, rich, plentiful life. However, somehow I lost track of this as I got caught up with life. As you know, I did not start off that way, as I was intent on living God's Word to the max. But one day I found myself battered and bruised by the very life I was pursuing. And boy, did all that stuff take its toll on me! Why?

Because somewhere down the line, I had taken a wrong turn. I had steered off track and wandered far from living the prosperous life God had promised. I had chosen a path that seemed wise to me and followed the masses. In my desire to be all that God had created me to be, I had traded His plan for me, His daughter, for a worldly recipe of disaster. If only I had slowed down. If only I had taken time out. Only then would I be still enough to see the woman I had become – hardened and weathered by the life I pursued.

I am not sure what would have happened to me had God not started ruffling my feathers and getting into my business; but thankfully, He did! He had His way of getting my attention. In my sprinting through life at colossal speeds, I had not stopped to consider what was going on inside me. But I realised I had a problem with the pace of my life when I found myself working 20-hour days.

I remember one incident when I had planned a much-needed three-week vacation. Most people would have stopped working a day or so before — well, at least the night before! Oh no, not me. And so there I was at 2:15 a.m. sitting in front of my computer, trying to finish a proposal, with a taxi booked for 3:00 a.m. The only problem was that I had not even packed! Can you believe that? My only saving grace was the fact that I had been throwing (literally) bits 'n' pieces into a suitcase all week along with my passport, travel documents and my credit card.

When I finally started my vacation, I had time to reflect. I began to ask myself where I was running to and what I was running from. What was so important that it was worth jeopardising the needs of my soul – no less my body and my spirit? Sister, this was my wake-up call. Needless to say, God got into my business and started to turn my attention inward as opposed to outward.

I can tell you, it's fantastic doing great things, succeeding and whatnot, but it is also equally important that no aspect of your life suffers *en route*. In this book, I focus on our emotional well-being because constantly *being and doing* will eventually take its toll on even the strongest among us. Simply put, there has to be "me time" — some downtime to deal with negative emotions that have cropped up over time. In addition to that, we need time to deal with the life situations constantly thrown at us, as well as taking time to deal with the emotional baggage we may have been carrying around.

Guess what? This is your "me time." I'd like you to consider this book a health resort or spa for your soul. So put your feet up and get ready for change!

Maybe you're wondering, *"So how do I deal with all of this emotional stuff you have been going on about?"* Or maybe you are wondering what emotional stuff I am rattling on about.

Great questions! They show that your heart is open. Moreover, God had you in mind when He commissioned this book. As you read on, you'll find some valuable lessons I learned that set me on my personal journey to emotional wholeness. These are based on my in-depth search of God's Word for principles, truths, strategies and promises for everyday living. Regardless of your background or beliefs, these are applicable to every human on earth. Moreover, God's Word has not changed. It still has the power to bring healing, deliverance and restoration for your soul.

Are you ready to be free from the emotional entanglements that have held you back or tripped you up time and time again? Are you keen to be the woman God has created you to be as opposed to a hybrid version of you? Do you desire to live the abundant life you know you were created to live? If you answered "yes" to any one of these, let's begin the journey.

PART 1

Preparation For Your
Journey To Emotional Wholeness

Chapter One

What's All The Fuss About?

Remember how I grew up wanting an abundant life in every facet of my life? That desire stayed with me for a long time – until I got caught up in the rat race. At that point, I no longer gave myself permission to slow down and take account of what was going on in my emotional life. My focus was locked onto a few things: success, accomplishing my goals, fulfilling my purpose and my relationship with God. It was a case of tunnel vision for me. Everything else took a back seat.

In my early days in the rat race, my spiritual life didn't suffer as much as my emotional life. At first, I had a few roles and responsibilities in my home church. For me, living a double-standard Christian life was simply not acceptable. I was determined to practice what I preached — especially since I knew that, someday, I would have to give an account of my life before the judgement throne. This kept me rooted and grounded in the Word and I carved out copious quiet times to talk to God.

Many years down the line, however, my sprinting lifestyle began to take its toll. It was becoming a burden, trying to juggle all the differing balls. I knew my cup was running over the brim with the stuff I kept shrugging to the side, but I kept on going. Soon enough, I believe my busy lifestyle became somewhere for me to hide, though this was not a conscious decision. I could bury myself in a zillion tasks, lend myself to loads of projects or even help others. By doing this, I never stood still, let alone had time to reflect. I think I gave new meaning to the word "busy". How wrong I was! How could I have skipped over the parts in the Bible where we read that even God rested and Jesus took time out regularly? It amazes me today that I never considered this. At any rate, I continued to plod along, juggling my personal, professional and church responsibilities and commitments. My faith in God never grew weary, but my soul sure did!

I never stood still, let alone had time to reflect. I think I gave new meaning to the word "busy".

As for my physical well-being, thankfully (by the grace of God) my body did not collapse under the ridiculous load I was carrying and the pressure I subjected it to. But I was physically shattered, because I had a habit of simply shrugging off tiredness when there was work to be done.

"Sleep and rest can wait until I finish this one thing..." was my sentiment. However, as you and I know, it is never just one thing. And so in retaliation, my body chose to stay a size 16 (14 to y'all in the USA) for the best part of a decade, regardless of what I did. It went on strike when it came to losing weight. I don't blame it. It was probably not sure of the next time I intended to eat or rest, so it held on to all it could.

In addition to this, two other factors came into play. First, there was a time when I was working abroad during the week. This meant eating in restaurants every night! Some might consider this a blessing, as all expenses were paid, but I can tell you, it takes its toll on your waistline and hips!

When I flew back home on Fridays, my food preparation followed a rigid philosophy that said anything that took more than 10 minutes to prepare was too much hard work. I'm sorry, but I could not be bribed (even with chocolate) to stand up in my kitchen and cook on a Friday night.

Second, I was also a full-fledged member of the comfort-eating club. Anyone who has been a member of this unofficial club of sisters will appreciate that our appetites are not the only things that drive us to eat. A bad day can do the trick — so can feeling isolated and unloved.

That takes us to my emotional life. Well, let's just say it did not look too good. My constant *being* and *doing* meant I had not checked in with my soul for the longest time. It was hard to say what I was harbouring inside. But you know what? God has a way of getting your attention. It's amazing how He designed our complex beings. God graciously built in a mechanism of emotional symptoms, which include negative emotions and behaviours.

Simply put, these mechanisms indicate to us that something isn't right within our beings. They work like physical symptoms that indicate to us when our bodies aren't in perfect working order. Just like physical symptoms, if emotional symptoms are ignored, they can lead to other complications. A few symptoms cropped up for me about this time — like my love-hate relationship with chocolate, a stinking attitude that surfaced periodically, and a compulsion to constantly work even in my down time.

What did I do with these emotional symptoms? I either brushed them aside or eventually convinced myself that that was just the way

God made me. Yeah, right! Of course, I found no evidence in the Bible that God had made anybody with a compulsion to work or love-hate feelings about chocolate. So I continued to brush the symptoms aside.

However, I soon developed a personal dissatisfaction with brushing aside the obvious in my life. For some reason, I could not bear living with these things day in, day out. Left alone, they had a tendency to trip me up once too often. You know how it is when you say to yourself, "I'm not going to do this again!" but minutes, hours, days, months or years later, you are back to square one? It matters not how many times you repent to God. Sooner or later, your emotional symptoms find their way right back into your life.

After living year in, year out like this, I found my emotional symptoms had become emotional baggage. And boy, was it tough trying to sprint through life with huge weights strapped to my ankles! Not only did these emotional weights slow me down, but at times, they brought me to a dead halt. I had targets and deadlines to meet, but I simply could not accomplish these with all the baggage I was dragging around.

Over time, my emotional symptoms didn't decrease, they increased! Life was throwing emotional stuff at me left, right and centre. And since I had not mastered the art of dealing with them, these emotional symptoms simply accumulated, joining their sister symptoms, like a stack of unopened mail. Yet I kept running and did not consider slowing down. Instead, I increased my efforts to compensate for the baggage I was carrying.

Strangely enough, when I started coaching, training and speaking to women, everywhere I went, I started noticing that other women were carrying emotional baggage just like me. They came in the form of clients, delegates and audience members. But it did not stop there. I shook their hands as they came into church. I sat next to them on planes and trains. They were on the pulpits and podiums of life — at gatherings, at networking events, in schools, on TV, on the pages of glossy magazines and newspapers. They were easy for me to recognize because, as they say, it takes one to know one!

It was as if we were all carrying the "*eb*" (emotional baggage) designer label. Our emotional baggage was carried in chic little handbags, medium-sized bags, overnight bags or huge trunks — depending on how much stuff we were dragging around with us. And of course, since our emotional baggage had become such a trendy accessory, no one raised an eyebrow. So many of us had at least one of these fashionable items accessorizing our lives, it simply became positively chic!

There was no question of who could afford it. It was available to all. Age, background, position, culture, religion and other demographics were no barriers to owning this designer label because, unlike the fashions found in high society, the "*eb*" designer label was free. We could all have as much emotional baggage as we liked.

The sad thing about this emotional baggage was that, no matter where we went or what we did professionally, spiritually, financially or emotionally, our baggage faithfully showed up too!

When I think of emotional baggage, some old movies spring to mind as useful analogies. You know those movies where a person is placed in a witness-protection program, their identity is changed, and they are relocated to some obscure part of the world, all for the purpose of protecting them from some notorious mobsters? Have

&

The sad thing about this emotional baggage was that, no matter where we went or what we did professionally, spiritually, financially or emotionally, our baggage faithfully showed up too!

&

you noticed that in a number of these movies, though the relocation was carefully and secretly planned, the bad guys seemed to track them down anyway? Strange, isn't it? I mean, on the surface, all the right things had been done, their tracks had been covered, and new identities had been assigned with no contact to their past. Simply put, a new life had been created. However, the bad guys always seemed to catch up with them, sooner or later.

Well, it's the same with emotional issues. You can apparently clean up your life, change jobs, relocate, change friends, remarry, rededicate your life to the Lord, but you can bet your bottom dollar that your old travel partners (or should I say, fashion accessories) sooner or later will catch up with you. They must have homing devices attached to them or something, because they always find their way back to Mama! So here you are thinking, "I'm free at last!" But your celebrations are cut short when your exclusive designer baggage reappears. Needless to say, your baggage resumes its long-time role of interfering with your life, making you act in ways contrary to the real you. This is because the real issue has not been dealt with.

Personally, this was my struggle for many years. Soon enough, my trendy designer baggage became a burden. The fact that I was soaring in all other aspects of my life was irrelevant. The simple truth remained that I could only get so far before my emotional baggage became an obstacle. I mean, have you tried leading or managing a group of people or even starting your own business while carrying emotional baggage? Have you tried pursuing God with all your heart, only to have your efforts marred by the baggage you've been carrying? Sooner or later, it eventually weighs you down. All your great intentions and efforts come to a halt as you struggle to carry so much emotional baggage.

This was the state of my life; that is, until God stepped in and began to reform me into the woman I was created to be. I tell you, it took awhile, but I did get onto my own journey of eliminating the emotional baggage in my life. And guess what? I was able to trade in my designer luggage for a life of inner tranquillity. Now, that's not to say that every so often the old gremlins won't try to resurface in moments of weakness; but the fact remains that we have God on our side and with Him, we can overcome whatever it is that we may face. And that is the real secret – *with Him!*

While God was teaching me these lessons, I learned that my problem wasn't really related to my environment, even though environments can have a great influence on us. Logic tells us that changing our environments in some way will solve the problem. So we try changing some aspect of our external being in order to fend off our emotional issues. But that's nothing more than trying to fix the situation by your own abilities.

If only that worked! Could you imagine the children of Israel trying to part the Red Sea by themselves? What if the woman with the issue of blood, who had been bleeding for twelve years, decided she was going to stick with her self-help methods to heal herself? We all know from the story that it took a touch of God to heal her. Otherwise, she may have bled to death.

Get the picture? You may not think our emotional baggage is as gigantic or problematic as being faced with the task of splitting of the Red Sea or a twelve-year bleeding disorder, but I beg to differ. These are all problems that need a higher power to solve. Just as jumping into the sea or spending your life seeking futile help can kill you, so emotional baggage can have a detrimental effect on your life that might lead to premature death.

When it comes to emotional baggage, we have to realise a few things.

1. It is not something you can eradicate by yourself without God. You see, you can do all the things human wisdom suggests, but it

takes God's wisdom and power to set you free for good — so you get no after-show re-appearances! If you were able to do it on your own, you wouldn't be looking in this book for help.

2. The sooner you realise that your issues, which make up your emotional baggage, go a lot deeper than what you see and know, the sooner you can be healed.

Bear in mind that your emotional issues are deep-seated within you. In the same way a tree starts off as a seedling and years later develops into a tree, so you may find that some of your issues may span way back into your childhood. Trying to push over a tree that has roots as deep as its height is not a small matter. The same is true for the emotional baggage that has sunk its roots deeply into your life.

I am not by any means saying all emotional baggage stems from childhood or that it is all so complex that it would take a monumental effort to uproot. What I am saying is that, whether your emotional baggage is one little bitty thing, one gigantic thing or a whole forest of things, get God involved.

Another point to bear in mind is that, depending on what your emotional issues are, I suggest you get the necessary support in the form of a godly group, community, and/or counsellor to support you along the way. I used the word *godly* since there are all sorts of groups, communities and professionals out there who can lead you astray. You need someone who is God-centred. After all, you are seeking them for help.

Now that I have mentioned the term *emotional issues*, let me give you my definition of what an emotional issue is.

By issue, I mean *any form of belief, attitude or behaviour you embrace — whether directed at yourself or others — that hinders the full expression of the person God has created you to be and results in the possible damage, degeneration or impeding of your emotional development and your overall well being.*

Emotional issues can be caused through self-infliction (harm we do to ourselves) and external infliction (harm done to us by others). Emotional symptoms are a result of emotional issues. These symptoms make us sit up and be aware that all is not well within our souls. A smart woman would take note of this and do something about it.

WHO IS THIS BOOK FOR?

This book is for every woman who is sick and tired of pretending everything is OK when she knows full well, deep down inside, that it's not. It's for the woman who...

1. is fed up with her emotional baggage influencing her every step, tripping her up or hindering her ability to live a normal life.
2. has been sprinting through life without taking the time to nurture her weathered soul.
3. has been battered and bruised by the very life she has pursued.
4. has been carrying around a lot of hurt from painful experiences which may have resulted in her crying (externally or deep within her soul).
5. has been wearing a mask all these years, too afraid for others to see the contortions of pain on her face.
6. has lived a non-authentic life, dancing to the tunes of others and pretending to be someone she is not.
7. has built a wall around herself and/or has developed other coping behaviours just to get through another day.
8. has a real desire to be truly happy, fulfilled and experience emotional freedom but has experienced everything else but this.

If you can relate to any of the above, this book is for you. It matters not what you have accomplished in the past, your current status, background and so on.

Personally, I got tired of living this way. I'm sure you feel the same way too! Because after awhile, it costs you more energy to keep your boat afloat with all this stuff hanging on to you. If you are ready to put all that behind you to live a baggage-free, truly joyful, fulfilled, prosperous and meaningful life, I believe you will find this book useful in steering you back on track to the path our heavenly Father set out for you. I believe when we eliminate all the emotional baggage we carry around with us, only then do we have the freedom to soar and accomplish great things.

So if you have been struggling with your thoughts, emotions, relationships, weight/food, personal aspirations and the like, get ready for change. I am really hoping that willingness on your part will allow the Spirit of God to make the mental and spiritual shifts necessary to change the foundations on which your beliefs, preconceptions, attitudes and behaviours are built.

I have written this book for Christians and non-Christians alike. Though women from all walks of life will benefit this book, I believe this book is invaluable to two particular types of women.

The first are those I call *pioneering women*. It may be that you have reached what you believe to be the peak of your success as you may have several accomplishments, have soared in your career, run a successful organisation, have huge responsibilities, lead a large number of people and are in the public eye.

The second group of women are *the pioneers-to-be women*. If you are this type of woman, you are going places. You have not yet reached your peak, but you are on your way.

Please note that neither of these lists is exhaustive, nor do they intend to ostracize other amazing women. It's my hope that all women who read this will consider this book worth having in their library.

In my line of work as a coach and consultant, however, I have made a sad discovery. Some women become almost obsessive about accomplishing goals, succeeding and being seen to be successful. The notion of succeeding is not a crime; but when it becomes the sole reason for one's existence or causes one to leave behind other areas of her life, this is where it causes a problem for women.

We often get so entangled in succeeding that God has no room to maneuver us off this treacherous and, at times, perilous course. We no longer give Him the room to call the shots in our lives or to lead us, as we cling blindly to our own agendas. I have been there and I know that being out of God's will is a lonely and difficult path.

Other women seem to be driven to prove themselves and their worth in a "man's world." So much so that they spend their lives trying to play catch up, excel beyond the odds, make a folly out of statistics and prove to the world they have what it takes. The problem is that they often pay a high price for this. They neglect investing in their spirits and souls, as these are no longer priorities. What these women don't seem to realise is that if they were to invest in these pertinent areas of their beings, they would eradicate the need to expend all the energy they are using to compensate for their lack of self-investment. We will look at both of these problems in detail later in the book.

Whoever you are, wherever you are in your life, I say, "Slow down … and enjoy the ride to emotional freedom." In the following chapters, I will be sharing some powerful principles along with life-changing mental and spiritual shifts I picked up in my One-to-one healing sessions with my heavenly Father. These will support you on your journey as you strive to accomplish all God desires for your life. They will support you in building a healthier, more solid foundation on which you can build all aspects of your life.

If there is any notion you will take away from this book, it is the fact that it is God's plan for you to live a wholesome life, so that you will be fit for service and avoid the roller-coaster effects of your emotional issues on your life.

EXPECT THE EXTRAORDINARY

To support you throughout this book, I will serve as your coach with the aim of achieving the following: imparting knowledge to help you cultivate healthy beliefs, attitudes and behaviours and, of course, inspiring you to action.

Personally, I have always valued having my own team of coaches and experts around to help me accomplish business-related projects, opportunities or challenges. This is in addition to my resident experts/senior management team — my heavenly Father, Jesus and the Holy Spirit.

I instigated this whole support network awhile back, when it suddenly dawned on me that I was not in fact a superwoman who could do all things. (And even if I could, my mission in life was not to be "all things to all men".) Having my two-pronged support approach, which gave me the best of both worlds, helped me in accomplishing my objectives. Therefore, you might find value also in adopting this approach in your life, as I am sure your intention is to live your best life.

Throughout this book, I shall be uncovering a number of concepts with the hope of supporting you in overcoming your emotional baggage. These are simply life-changing principles that have helped me, along with many others, free ourselves from the traps our emotional baggage sets out for us.

As your coach, my utmost desire is to see change in your life. I don't know about you, but I am tired of reading books or attending conferences, getting all excited for a short period of time and then reverting back to my previous state. I am sure you have experienced that too.

I want more out of my life than temporary change. I want permanent change, so I can be all God wants me to be and live the life He wants me to live. That's why I made God the centre of this book, as He is the only One capable of bringing about permanent change. Therefore, this journey we're about to take together requires that you determine in your heart that you will not be returning to the status quo. I know Rome was not built in a day; but as long as your heart's desire is for change, I believe God will honour that. All you need to do is prepare your heart and walk hand in hand with Him.

To provide you with further help, I have incorporated a number of concepts I have called *Journaling Moments, Praying Moments, Enlightening Moments* and *Healing Moments*. As your coach, I encourage you to spend time on these. I do strongly suggest that you don't just skip over these sections, but take time out to really reflect.

I would rather you spent longer on this book, chewing and digesting all the meaty nuggets served up than that you skim it and find it makes little or no difference in your life. That would be a waste of your time. The material was put together to make you stop, think and take action. Anything less than this would be a futile action on your part.

I have also included a number of biblical references that enforce certain points for you to mull over. I find this a powerful aid because the more you delve into God's Word, the more you discover about Him and what He has in mind for you, His precious daughter. Without His Word, there simply is no other way to accomplish this.

And so, my request to you is that you take time out, slow down and use the book as an aid to reflect on your life. There will be times when I will try to invoke a response, change an attitude, behaviour, or create a mental shift in your thinking. There may even be some challenging moments, but it's nothing a strong woman like you can't handle. By all means, make entries into your own journal in regard to what comes up for you as you read. This is often useful in capturing thoughts that you can peruse later.

In short, the contents of this book will be an aid to you in becoming emotionally restored in God's way. If this is something you would like to accomplish, then read on.

I pray that the principles found in this book will impact your life, as they have done in mine. Without further ado, let's begin the journey.

JOURNALING MOMENT

Write down what you are hoping this book will support you in accomplishing.

_____

_____

_____

_____

_____

_____

Write down the areas of your life that you believe need to be restored. Use this section to note the emotional baggage you have been carrying.

_____

_____

_____

_____

_____

_____

_____

Chapter Two

Mental Shifts: Mental Preparation For Your Journey

hances are that you have picked up this book in an attempt to deal with some of the excess baggage you have been carrying. Maybe it has come to light through the negative emotions or emotional symptoms you experience. Like many other women, you have a desire to be free from the junk that has hindered you from being real, being your best and living your best life.

It's not that you have not tried to eradicate them. In fact, in an effort to overcome them, you may have tried a number of temporary remedies to "fix" yourself. The result? Simply put, nothing much has changed, as you keep going round and round in circles — ending up right back where you started. Moreover, you're still carrying your mess! If you are anything like me, you may have thought that your do-it-yourself (DIY) temporary fixes had cured you — except for the fact that, under certain circumstances or in response to certain triggers, you always relapse back to square one. Perhaps you've simply gotten frustrated and tired of searching for healing for your damaged soul.

Whatever your story, I say, "Read on, Sister!"

Let me start off by commending you in recognizing your need and being willing to do something about it. Not everyone is courageous enough to do both.

Remember I said that this book is all about mental and spiritual shifts? Well, I would like to prepare you mentally for this journey by stating a few truths that you *will* need to embrace to get the best out of this book. It's not rocket science. These truths are based on biblical principles. Before I delve into them, I would like to frame your mind with this wonderful verse from four different versions of the Bible:

> *When people do not accept divine guidance, they run wild. But whoever obeys the law is happy.*
>
> Proverbs 29:18

> *Where there is no revelation, the people cast off restraint; but happy is he who keeps the law.*
>
> Proverbs 29:18, NKJV

> *Where there is no vision, the people perish: but he that keepeth the law, happy is he.*
>
> Proverbs 29:18, KJV

> *If people cannot see what God is doing, they stumble all over themselves; but when they attend to what He reveals, they are most blessed.*
>
> Proverbs 29:18, MSG

I have intentionally used a number of versions of the Bible so you can get the essence of the verse. Personally, I have taken the verse to mean that any time I deviate from God and His Word, I am asking for trouble. Simple! The reason is that there is safety, provision, healing, direction, nourishment and much more in His Word. And if I am to be completely honest, a number of situations in my life could have been avoided if I had clung to the truth I knew.

So I want to set the scene of the book by sharing five principles or home truths this Sister had to take on board, digest and internalise along her journey. I call these *The Five Principles To Living An Abundant Life.* These five principles can be applied to all other areas of your life as they were designed to support you in living the abundant life — which encompasses realised potentials, personal effectiveness, purposeful living, personal fulfilment, lasting success and much more. However, we will be looking at these five principles from the context of our subject – emotional well-being.

THE FIVE PRINCIPLES TO LIVING AN ABUNDANT LIFE

Principle One: Get God Involved Right From The Start

There comes a time when we must accept the fact that it is only when we get God involved in our life situations that we will overcome or accomplish things — especially those things that appear insurmountable to us. God is an expert at getting things done, turning around situations and making the impossible a reality. He never intended our fragile shoulders to carry the huge burdens we traipse around with. We are to cast them unto Him, according to First Peter 5:7 which says:

Give all your worries and cares to God, for he cares about what happens to you.

Dealing with our emotional baggage is not exempt from this rule, either. After all, God has proven to be great at sorting out anything from minor issues to huge, boulder-like, show-stopping issues that can perturb our lives. This principle comes into play regardless of whether you seek professional help and godly counselling or not. God is still the Ultimate Healer. It might help to see Him as your Creator — the Master Engineer who created you and holds the blueprints of your life. He knows exactly what knobs to twiddle. He knows all there is to know about you. No one else can or will ever know you as God knows you. After all, His Word says He has numbered the hairs on your head (Matthew 10:30). Who else do you know who takes the time to do something as tedious as that? God created you for a specific purpose; it is your responsibility to build a relationship with Him to discover the course for your life. Unfortunately, many people, even Christians, omit this part and think they can make it going solo.

How much better it is to make God the centre of your life and hand over all things, including your emotional restoration, to Him. To make God the centre of your life means you will need to get to know Him by reading His Word, incorporating His teachings into your everyday life and communicating with Him through prayer – in a consistent manner, if I may say so!

Principle Two: Learn To Connect With Others

Overcoming emotional damage is not a DIY job or something you should try to tackle in isolation. In fact spiritual, physical and emotional isolation are huge contributory factors as to why many of us end up carrying our baggage for as long as we do. It's no wonder our emotions are up the creek.

You will need to adopt something I term *external association*, which is a connection between you and others spiritually, physically and emotionally. To do this means you must first build a relationship with God, your heavenly Father (a spiritual connection), as I mentioned in Principle One.

Secondly, rather than isolating yourself, as many of us tend to do, you should consider looking for godly professionals, counsellors, groups or friends who can support you. You may want to consider reading this book in your book club or in the company of other like-minded, trustworthy and loving women (a physical and emotional connection). God did not create us to be isolated from Him or His other created beings. This has been one truth I have had to learn the hard way!

Principle Three: Take Time To Develop Yourself

In order to bring your emotions back to restoration, you will also need to adopt what I term *internal association,* which is a connection within your own tripartite being (i.e., your spirit, soul and body). No aspect of your innate being was created to function in isolation from the others, because they need one another to function effectively.

For instance, by developing your spirit through building a relationship with God,

> ✿
>
> *No aspect of your innate being was created to function in isolation from the others, because they need one another to function effectively.*
>
> ✿

you will start to develop a healthy awareness of who you are and why you are here. Your heart and mind will use this information to set internal standards, rules, values, beliefs and attitudes, which will drive your behaviours to help you accomplish your mission. By taking care of your physical body, too, you will be able to go off and do the things you believe were created to do.

However, in our driven societies, many people leave certain aspects of their beings behind for the pursuit of others. This is why you can find a woman who has an incredible body — because she works out and eats right (or eats nothing!) — but discover that she has omitted to invest the same amount of effort in nourishing and developing her spirit and soul. There are so many women who dress in the latest trendy items, but forget to dress their spirits with godly principles. Other women place a heavy emphasis on becoming successful in their career, yet fail to place an equivalent emphasis of success on other aspects of their lives.

When we place more emphasis on one aspect of our beings at the jeopardy of the rest of our beings, we risk becoming what I call *lopsided women,* who on the surface look great — physically, financially and successfully — but are not doing as well emotionally and spiritually. All too often, their inner beings have been emaciated or depleted of nourishment. These women often look to the media, magazines, fads and other people's words or behaviours to guide their lives. Sooner or later they use this information to determine their identities, worth and purpose on earth.

In the long run, a woman like this finds that her body becomes a house to a number of dead things — such as lost identity, dead dreams, wasted talents, a contaminated heart and emotional baggage. She soon resembles what Jesus termed "whitewashed tombs - beautiful on the outside but filled on the inside with dead people's bones and all sorts of impurity" (Matthew 23:27). In this state, she is susceptible to addictions, compulsive and impulsive behaviours and a whole raft of things, due to the state of her inner being. After all, she has no internal defence to propel her out of this.

What I mean by internal defence is a solid foundation in biblical principles. These are akin to the internal defences of our body's immune system that fights and protects us from attacks. You know what happens when your natural immune system is weakened? You are more prone to more diseases than someone with a healthy immune system. And so, something as simple as an infection could jeopardise your life.

Just in case you are thinking, "I have made it through life without God or nurturing my inner being!" I would ask you this: "Have you really?"

I guess it depends what you define as "made it." I don't know about you, but what I gather — from both my own life and that of other women I have worked with — tells a different story. Women who omit to develop certain parts of their being are prone to living unfulfilled, unhappy, hopeless or purposeless lives. Because of a busy lifestyle or ignorance, they have not paid attention to their entire beings. The sustenance they could have gained from feeding on God's Word is lacking and they have ended up feeding on whatever the surrounded area — the media, their family, their friends and society — dishes out.

I have lost track of the number of women I have come across over the years who do not appreciate who they are, what their gifts and talents are, what their values, their needs and even their likes and dislike are! In coaching conversations, when I ask them these questions along with what they would like to do with their lives, the answer is often "I don't know."

Now while I appreciate that some of us are late bloomers, I believe God prepares us for our callings by sowing little seeds here and there. So while you may not know the full picture, He gives you something to work on. However, it is very easy to lose sight of these things in this day and age where our upbringing, education, employers, society – to say the least — seem intent on moulding us into something we aren't. Couple this with not building your relationship with God, and it's no wonder so many women are living in limbo.

The thing that disheartens me the most is the fact that many women have gone through a significant portion of their lives without knowing why they are here and have settled for simply existing as replicas of someone else! You have only to watch TV or look to the glossy magazines to see the clones appearing.

There are so many implications in failing to connect with your real self. I believe if people have lost touch with who they are for a long time, they have been surviving on "junk food". They may have learned ways of coping with their situation and give the impression that they have "made it" through their accomplishments. They may even associate their accomplishments with their identity. But they do not have the first clue as to who they really are and what their purpose on this earth might be.

This is a place where I personally was stuck. So I know it is quite easy to think that producing results is an indication that you are being who you ought to be. Can I just let you in on a secret? You do realise that you can have huge accomplishments and yet fail woefully in other areas of your life, don't you? If you don't believe me, look around our society today.

Principle Four: Don't Settle Where You Are

Regardless of how you look at your situation, God never intended for you to remain the way you are — trapped by your emotional baggage. This contradicts His own Word.

Remember earlier, I kept emphasizing the fact that I was bent on living the abundant life, as in John 10:10. Another version of this verse talks about "life in all its fullness" (NLT). Either way, it indicates the kind of life God intended for us.

God wants us to continue to strive to develop all aspects of our lives and not just settle for mediocrity. God wanted this so much for us that He sent His only Son to die for our sins, giving us the opportunity to live the fullness of life He has promised us. In trying to accomplish this, Jesus spent time His time on earth 1) changing people's beliefs, mindsets, and behaviours (emotional restoration), 2) healing people's bodies (physical restoration) and 3) restoring people's relationships with God (spiritual restoration).

I believe the aim of all this was to bring us back in line with God's desires for us and empower us with the ability to strive for more. God's plan has not changed since then and is still relevant for us today. So if you think that the way you are is simply your lot in life or the way things were meant to be, I say, "Think again, Sister!" You couldn't be more wrong.

Weren't you made in the image of God? (Genesis 1:26-27) So far, I have not come across a mediocre God, carrying around with Him emotional baggage. Therefore, I suggest you get rid of notions like, "This was how God created me."

While I appreciate that many of us have been through some tough ordeals, I still believe that we can overcome them and live extraordinary lives. Sister, it's time to move into emotional freedom!

Principle Five: Focus On Your Purpose, Not Your Agenda!

Now many of you go-getting, highflying Sisters out there might just be squirming in your seats right now…and that's cool. I hear you loud and clear, because I squirmed when the reality of this hit me. I thought, "You mean to tell me that I cannot do all those things I want to do?" That was my initial thought, because this Sister had loads of things she wanted to get done. And it was hard to accept that I had to let go of some of the things I was clutching so tightly.

Later on, I got an understanding of this principle. It isn't that God wants to cramp our styles or be a party-pooper. On the contrary! However, we do have a tendency to preoccupy ourselves and cloud our visions with a lot of nonessential things. It's not to say that these aspirations are immoral; but once we get our teeth into something we perceive as being good, some of us have a tendency of pursuing it to the detriment of ourselves and our main purpose here on earth.

This brings me to the second point of our individual purposes. We are all here on earth for a purpose, regardless of where we may find ourselves today. Just because you have a qualification or have learned to do certain things exceptionally well, it is not necessarily an indication that you are living purposefully. I know that this statement may make some people disgruntled, but it is the truth.

Over the years, I have gained a vast amount of experience doing different things, which I have learned to be good at. But looking back today, I know that using the expert knowledge or qualifications I gained were not my main purpose. While they could help me along the way, it would have been a bad move to follow a particular career without further guidance from God. After all, He is my Employer! If I were to base my purpose on what I excelled at or what I thought I had a flair for, I doubt very much that you would be reading this book today.

Have you noticed how empty you feel inside when you get caught up in this malarkey? Sister, life is too short for that!

Recognising that you have a higher calling demands that you recognize the fact that you simply cannot afford to lug around with you your emotional baggage while trying to be effective in your mission. It also means that you cannot live your life as you choose. You have an obligation to fulfil.

The only problem is that many of us get caught on the treadmills or rat race of life, trying to fulfil our own agendas. Or we do things on the side, in addition to what we ought to be focusing on. We get so busy with all this that, in the process we lose focus, get burned out, stressed and amass emotional baggage.

Have you noticed how empty you feel inside when you get caught up in this malarkey? Sister, life is too short for that! God did not create you for the purpose of merely chasing futile dreams (i.e., any dream outside of God's plan for you). You were created to accomplish His plans.

og

These five principles are the foundation stones on which I built this book. If you are struggling to get to grips with these life-changing truths, I suggest you simply take some time out to consider why, as it is so imperative to grasp them. They will need to move from your head to your heart, for it is your heart that affects all that you do (Proverbs 4:23). When this happens, it will enable you to adopt godly and healthy mindsets.

These principles have been gleaned from the Bible. As you may know, the Bible consists of eternal truths that will always be applicable till the end of time. So once again, consider your reasons for resisting principles that stand to change your life forever. And let's face it. The chances are, you have tried other ways and have found yourself in the same predicament. So what have you got to lose?

On my own personal journey in seeking emotional restoration, I discovered that man-based solutions (solutions devised by men that don't point people in the direction of God, their Creator) don't work or have lasting results. Take, for example, the notion of self-help. Though there are a number of useful and motivating notions out there, we need to recognise that it's God Almighty Who can bring lasting change.

Think about it; if we mere mortals could really help ourselves, there would be no need for God. In fact, you would have resolved your own emotional issues a long time ago and be living an abundant life, full of fulfilment, internal joy, success and purpose.

Take a moment to consider this: If humans were really able to deal with their own messes, then why is the world in the state it is today? Getting more information certainly won't help. After all, there has never been as much information being shared as there is today. Makes you think, doesn't it? If we truly had the answers, our societies would be better places to live. Personally, I think we have lost the plot by seeking self-sufficiency. That's not the way God ordained things to be.

So, please do not see this book as a self-help guide. Rather, it's my intent to point you to your heavenly Father Who has the power to help you. Therefore, I would like you to do a quick mental shift and set your mind on seeking God's help. I know this may be a hard pill to swallow, since many of us have been in the control seat of our own lives for a long time. However, I would encourage you to relinquish control to God and let the principles sink in for awhile.

Chapter Three

Spiritual Shifts: Spiritual Preparation For Your Journey

ow that we have looked at creating mental shifts, I thought it appropriate we look at creating *spiritual shifts* as well to aid you on this journey. As I've said, we are tripartite beings made up of a spirit, soul and body. All these facets of our beings are connected and help us function as human beings. You cannot have one without the others, as they all serve different functions. Nor can you choose to focus on one over the others without it having a detrimental impact on your entire being in the long run.

I know many people may want to argue this point and even stress the fact that they have survived all this while without a need for spiritual connection with God or all that "spiritual stuff." That's just my point – they have merely *survived!*

When God created mankind, He had no intention of having us merely survive. He created us to live abundant, fulfilled, wholesome and prosperous lives. This applies to every aspect of our lives.

So for those who have been flying solo without God or without an intimate relationship with Him, you might want to take a good look at all areas of your life. If you are being honest, you might have noticed that any periods away from God or in times you have not nourished your spirit were times you experienced a sense of deep longing on the inside. People have also been known to call this longing an emptiness. It's a state that occurs when your spirit becomes separate from God. That yearning is caused by an innate spiritual need that God placed inside each and every one of us.

I remember experiencing this feeling in my brief stint away from God in my college days. With my newfound freedom as a college student, miles away from home, I wanted to do things my way for awhile. However, despite being in the throng of college life, I felt alone and isolated. It was strange because I was surrounded by other students like me; I had made loads of friends and was having fun. However, I consistently felt like something crucial was missing from my life that even the best party on campus could not satisfy.

After what I can only describe as *missing God dearly*, I decided to find Him in my own way and I found my way back into His loving arms. Never again do I want to feel that sense of separation from my Creator! Many people who have joined the family of God can attest to the appeal of this approach of discovering God over a fear-driven, "hellfire and brimstone" approach.

Even while remaining Christians, many will, at some stage in their lives, drift away from God for various reasons. Again, the emptiness, yearnings and feelings of isolation will kick in, because God did not create us to live independently of Him. It is through our spirits that we connect and build our relationships with Him. Our connection opens the door for us to revere, worship, believe, hope and much more.

Ignorance, denial, or lack of comprehension about the emptiness does not get rid of this spiritual need. That's why we see many people adopting precarious methods of meeting it, such as participating in fads, addictive or irrational behaviours, and so on. A spirit not filled with God will become depraved, even when that is not the individual's original intention. Why? Because if you are not connected with God and do not fill your spirit with spiritual food, it will feed off of whatever is around.

One of the Bible stories I read as a child was about the Israelites in the wilderness. Moses had gone up the mountain for forty days to hear from God. Until that time, the Israelites had been accustomed to hearing from God. And now their spiritual leader had vanished — and they did not hear from God during that time. I believe it was in their effort to satisfy their spiritual need that they built a golden calf with the help of Aaron (Exodus 24:12-32:29). I have no doubt that their inability to connect with God created feelings of separation and isolation that drove them to create an object they could worship. In fact, throughout the Bible, we see the hearts of the Israelites straying away from God and turning their affections to other things in an attempt to fill their spirits. If we look at our world today, it looks like history repeating itself, with many hearts straying and looking for other objects of their affections.

Therefore, one of the spiritual shifts I would like you to acknowledge is the fact that we all have an inherent spiritual need to be connected to God and to be in constant union with Him.

This goes hand in hand with the subject of emotional restoration and links to the first two of the five principles I mentioned previously. Whichever way you look at it, God is the Creator of all things. Only He has the power to change your life – for good. Once you grasp this fact, you then need to take action, based on faith, to connect with Him.

Failing to do this is as bad as being stuck on a deserted island. In the near distance, you can see a lighthouse that illuminates the way for ships at night. Day in, day out, you see ships pass by being guarded by the light coming from the lighthouse. As the time goes by, your desire to leave the island increases, even though you have grown accustomed to the way of life on the island. And so you are faced with a few options: You can swim out to the lighthouse, make a raft, or build a fire to catch someone's attention. You could also simply stay where you are – deserted and alone on the island. The choice is truly yours.

WILL YOU ANSWER THE CALL?

Taking part in God's divine plan for abundant living, emotional healing and salvation requires you to believe in Jesus Christ. You need to be one of God's own to partake of all that He has stored for His children. When trying to explain this to people, I normally use the following analogy.

I have a set of keys to my parents' home, despite the fact that I do not live there. I am privileged to have these keys because I am their daughter. I am related and bound to them by blood. This means that I can have constant access to them. I can come and go as often as I like, especially in the times when I need help, food, shelter or love. Therefore, I possess these keys because I am their child.

Now what do you think would happen in the case of a complete stranger? Do you suppose the stranger would have the same access rights as I do, if any at all? Would a stranger have the same privileges as I do? The answer is no. They are unrelated to me or my parents. Remember, I belong to my parents, that's why I am entitled to rights a complete stranger does not have. The common bond that ties me together with my parents is absent with the stranger. And so, at best, all the stranger can do is peer through the windows, but not partake of what my parents provide for me.

This is the same with God. You must belong to Him, be in relationship with Him and be a part of His awesome family to enjoy the privileges of a child of God. This will then give you constant access to Him.

You may be wondering how you can be a part of this glorious family or rekindle your relationship with God. It's simple. Just ask Jesus Christ into your life. The Bible clearly tells us that there is no other name in heaven or earth whereby men must be saved (Acts 4:12). All you have to do is sincerely say the prayer below and invite Jesus Christ into your life as described in Romans 10:8-13. Remember that the handle to the door of your heart is on the inside; only you can open the door. Why not open the door today and let Jesus in by saying the prayer below?

PRAYING MOMENT

Dear Jesus,

I repent of my sins. I recognize You as my Lord and Saviour. I believe You died on the cross for me and rose again from the dead. Today, I invite You into my life. I ask that You become my Master and lead me each step of the way by Your Holy Spirit. I surrender my whole life to You and ask You to take control of it from this day on and forever more. Lord, make me a child that You will be proud of and help me in fulfilling the purpose You created me for.

In Jesus' name, Amen.

C３

If you have just said this prayer sincerely for the first time, congratulations! I would like to be the first to welcome you into the family of the God. This truly is the first step on your journey to living the life God has planned for you. If you have said the prayer after a stint away from God, I salute you and say, "Welcome home, Sister! I hope you can hear me cheering. We have been waiting for you. Great to have you back where you rightfully belong!"

To those who have already accepted Jesus Christ as their Lord and Saviour, thanks for being patient. I encourage you to delve deeper in your relationship with Him. Since we are all starting out on the same journey, there is no better time to build a deep and meaningful relationship with Him than now. So Sister, let's begin the journey to emotional wholeness. Hope your expectations are high!

Before I go on, I have one more request of you, my Sister. Let's invite our Father to join us on this incredible journey. Trust me; we will need all the help, guidance and comfort we can get. So in your own time, say the following prayer:

PRAYING MOMENT

Father,

I ask in the name of our Lord Jesus Christ that You hold me by the hand as I embark on this journey. I ask that You lead me to a place of complete healing, deliverance and restoration, in Jesus' name. I pray for healing — spiritually, physically and emotionally. I pray that I will find that place of peace, comfort and freedom from the emotional baggage and pain I have been carrying. I ask that the Holy Spirit, the true Comforter, will lead me to that perfect place that God has predestined for me. Father, I pray that You will grant me the strength and grace to complete the journey ahead of me.

Finally Father, I commit myself into Your precious hands and ask that You surround me with the blood of the Lamb and preserve me till the completion of Your mighty work in me. Perfect all that concerns me and make me a useful vessel for You.

In Jesus' mighty and awesome name, Amen.

PART 2

Understanding The Female Hybrid

Chapter Four

Characteristics Of The Female Hybrid

ecently I started to ponder where the real women God created might have gone. Many of us have been caught up with building our successful empires, making it to the top of our career ladders, accomplishing our own agendas, running the perfect homes and ministries, raising perfect kids, being perfect moms, wives, partners and even Christians — to list a few things.

As I have said before, these are not at all bad in themselves. My concern has always been the price we pay with our tripartite beings to accomplish these things. Accomplishing any of these aspirations by worldly standards — in other words, anything that appeals to the values of the world, but goes against the Word of God — will have a detrimental effect on us.

For example, our driven society today rarely affords men or women the time to get off the treadmill. Our busy days are so crammed with deadlines, targets, and mile-long to-do lists that we simply haven't got enough time in the day to slow down.

As I mentioned before, it took me a long time to bring back into focus how much the Bible talked about taking a rest. After all, even God rested! The only problem is that some of us cram in more work on our Sundays to play catch up. I would be the first to put my hand up to say I use weekends, including Sundays after church, to come to grips with mounting emails or meet deadlines. For some people, it may not be work, but church, family or other commitments that just can't seem to survive without you on Sundays.

However, God never meant for us to live like this. We were never meant to be constantly on the go, because the repercussions of the non-stop lifestyle are manifold. Burnout and stress are some of the first repercussions – not to mention a mangled emotional life, which is the crux of this book. There is also the danger of failing to fulfil our missions in life because we are not in any shape to do them. Some people are comforted by the fact that they have bursts of success here and there. But this is nothing compared to how you'll feel when your full potential is realised.

Our driven lives leave no room for failure, breakdowns, down time or healing that are part and parcel of life. To compensate, we just keep forging ahead at full speed, putting to the back of our minds our mounting pile of emotional issues. As a result, many of us are walking around wounded. This gives birth to negative emotions and behaviours.

The higher the mounting pile of emotional issues, the less we see of the women God had in mind when we were created. After all, our energies are tied up in keeping our boats afloat and giving the impression that all is well, when the reality is far from it. At this kind of pace, the real you simply does not have time to enter the equation.

I have to admit that by never staying still for long enough, I never got around to dealing with some of the emotional issues I picked up along the way. I was simply far too busy getting on with my goals and saving the world.

"But weren't you doing a lot of great stuff?" you may be wondering. Absolutely. I was doing loads of stuff that primarily benefited others. It was not all "me, me, me!" Sister, as far as I was concerned, I was doing God's work. Well, that was what I set out to do, anyway....

However, in my strivings to get it all done, I must have thought that doing all this great stuff for God meant living an unbalanced life, filled with stress and burnout. If I, like many others, had taken the time in the early days to truly walk with the Father through the Holy Spirit, I would not have gotten into the state I was in. Nowhere in the Bible does it say, "Thou must throw common sense out of the window and kill thyself spiritually, emotionally and physically in the process of serving God." The precious Word of God gives us light and illuminates our understanding. It helps us order our steps and follow the right path. The only problem is that many have strayed far from the path.

But I continued to run on full throttle ... at least until I ran out of steam and came grinding to a halt. At that point, I did whatever I could to relight the fire in my engine room, so I could get back on track and hit my deadlines. It was imperative that I resume my agenda.

Notice the words "my deadlines" and "my agenda"? So where did God's agenda go? Forget the fact that my soul had been sending out signals to caution me. I simply ignored them. Sister, it never occurred to me to call out to ask the Engineer to fix my faulty machinery or even hand myself over for major servicing. Oh no, I could not do that! What would people say if they thought all was not well with me? Could I really afford to be exposed in such a manner?

Worse still, getting God in my business would have meant I had to be still in His hands as clay is in the potter's hands. For me, being still was akin to doing absolutely nothing. Argggh! The words "doing nothing" were like swear words to me. I likened them to laziness, complacency, falling behind and 101 other things I did not want in my life. It was too costly to stop because that meant my tasks would start piling up. And so I carried on, like many others do.

The end result of this non-stop lifestyle, which does not allow you to get to grips with the real you, means you become the lopsided woman I mentioned. Certain parts of your being are not as well-developed as others. When this happens, we no longer get to see the original or real you. What we see is the proliferation of a hybrid version of ourselves — the *female hybrid*. The female hybrid is a fusion that combines two specific elements: the original woman God created (the authentic woman) and a counterfeit version of the original woman that has degenerated over time (the fake woman). More often than not, we see very little of the authentic woman. Over time, when her emotional baggage is not dealt with, we see even less of the authentic woman, who is now forced to the background.

I have come across several emerging patterns of this special breed of woman. The list below is not meant to be an exhaustive list. It simply contains some of the stronger patterns I have come across. It is also not meant to condemn women who exhibit these patterns. I merely offer it as a simple illustration of how a number of us have evolved over time.

> *The female hybrid is a fusion that combines two specific elements: the original woman God created (the authentic woman) and a counterfeit version of the original woman that has degenerated over time (the fake woman).*

THE FEMALE CLONE

By *female clone* I mean the woman who has lost her own internal sense of identity. She tells herself she likes what others like and always does what others do. She does not seem to have a mind of her own. Even if she did, it's gone A.W.O.L (absent without leave). What the world sees is a fake copy of the original woman — fake in the sense that we no longer see the original version or the essence of the woman she was created to be. She did not start out this way, but over time, something changed. I believe two things could have happened.

The first may be, she listened to the *external voices* of the people around her who told her that who she was wasn't good enough. Those who have authority over people are often guilty of wanting to clone the people in their care into replicas of themselves or someone completely different from the person God originally created. Those guilty of this include parents, leaders, managers, teachers and even pastors.

This woman may have had her individuality suppressed from childhood, when we would have seen her authentic self in full bloom. Over the course of her development to adulthood, outside sources such as friends, family, partners, media, tradition, culture, church and society at large could have contributed their penny's worth of rules and regulations on how this woman ought to believe, think, behave and live.

By listening to these external voices, she gradually pushes aside what she honoured and valued merely to conform, rather than be seen as a rebel by obeying her own *internal voice*. However, deep within her, the real woman still yearns to be expressed. Her yearnings are reflected by her discontentment with these external rules.

A good example of this is the little girl who has an artistic flair, but whose dreams of becoming an artist are quashed by the well-meaning adults in her life, the parents and teachers who suggest she opt for studying law, medicine or something equally pragmatic. If she complies, she will ultimately become a woman in her thirties who is probably doing well on the career path chosen for her — except that she hates every day she has to do anything but art.

The second reason someone becomes a female clone is by admiring — or even envying — someone else's gifts, talents and calling so much so that she decides to abandon her own calling to pursue the dream of that other person. You know how it is when you meet someone who is doing something that blows your mind. It's natural to think that what they are doing is so great that we want to do the same. The only problem is that the female clone never stops to check in with herself to ensure that that's what she is supposed to be doing with her life. And so she embarks on someone else's journey and spends a chunk of her life trying to live their dream. It may be a great dream; but it's not her true calling. So, again, the end result is an unfulfilled and purposeless life.

This female clone can choose to break free and follow her heart's desires to use her God-given talents (or at least find a way of using them) or she can stay put in her unfulfilling career path. Sadly, many female clones opt for the latter option – spending the remainder of their lives wondering what could have been. Sound familiar?

It helps to remember that clones are replicas of other people. In the real sense of the word, a clone is a carbon copy of whatever it is cloned from – right down to the DNA. However, have you noticed that God did not make any of us clones? We are all unique expressions and reflections of God.

THE FEMALE CHAMELEON

Even though the *female chameleon* bears an uncanny resemblance to the female clone, this hybrid differs in that chameleons blend in with the background in order to protect themselves. The female chameleon uses this blending technique to protect herself from the rejection and abandonment of others. So her aim is to constantly change herself, depending on what's going on around her, with the purpose of blending in with the crowd.

While the female clone still retains — or is, at least, aware of — what she values and believes, the female chameleon is different in that she constantly changes as her surroundings change. Hence, she adopts chameleon-like tendencies, such as changing the way she presents herself as she roams from church to church, job to job, relationship to relationship.

So as to blend in, the female chameleon takes on the role of an impersonator, since she has not thought through what she stands for. She impersonates people who make an impression on her – the good, the bad and the ugly. This woman tends to have many sides or personalities as well. Chameleons can act 101 different ways. She may have a "Praise the Lord! Hallelujah!" Christian Sister version of herself. Then there may be a secularised version of her so she can blend easily with the world, a girlfriend/wife version or a sister/daughter version and many more. This woman acts a part and tries to be "all things to all men." Living with this kind of person can be tough, as she keeps you guessing which side you will see next.

As with the female clone, when you peel back the layers, you might find a woman who has been rejected or abandoned. You might find a woman who was traumatised in her childhood by bullies who picked on her for being different than her peers. You might find a woman who, after several broken relationships with guys, has come to the conclusion that to get the love and affection she needs, she will sacrifice herself by being whatever her partner wants her to be. And the list goes on. Again, you can see how her need for love, affection or even attention has driven her to being a female chameleon.

THE FEMALE MASQUERADER

The *female masquerader* maintains an awareness of her own being and endeavors to avoid drawing attention to herself and being rejected by others when they find out more about her. Chances are that she has a few outstanding emotional issues that she has not dealt with. So, in order to save face, she comes to the conclusion that it is not safe to reveal her real self.

She learns to bottle up how she feels, then hides behind her personality, clothing, intelligence, activities, success and much more. This woman may be someone who is benevolent, successful and respected. By doing all the great stuff she does, she is able to project a certain aspect of herself whilst keeping the crux of herself hidden. Her safeguard is to keep busy and keep her real self away from the public eye. It is as if she lives in a world which is a perpetual masquerade ball, where all the attendees wear masks. The only difference is that her mask is permanently on whenever she is in the public eye.

Behind the scenes, it's a different story. Though she is able to keep up a front in public, she may have found herself a safe haven where she can temporarily take off her mask until she performs again. This safe haven could be her bedroom or bathroom. Wherever it is, it exists behind closed doors. In this place, you will probably find her crying copiously. She can let herself cry because it's behind the scenes. No one will ever know.

Because of our complex nature as humans, she would also have developed a coping behaviour to temporarily meet her needs. And so she may have developed compulsive/impulsive behaviours, addictions (e.g., food, alcohol and/or sex), or regressive behaviours, such as going back to a childhood behaviour that brought her comfort. Whatever she adopts, it is meant to get her through the night seasons of her life, so she can make it through another day.

THE FEMALE SUPERHERO

Without this *female super hero,* our world will simply crumble – or so she thinks. She is the only reason why her marriage is still going strong, her ministry is thriving, her career is booming, her family's needs are met — the list is endless.

As far as she is concerned, she is indispensable to the rest of us. We need her! And so, because of our needs, she puts on her superhero outfit each day to go out there and save the world – including those who don't know they have to be saved or don't even want to be saved. This kind of woman is often stressed and close to burnout, if she is not already there. She may lack solid boundaries (i.e., she can't say "no" to a person in need) and, more than likely, she has no support mechanism in place to meet her own needs.

Over time, she becomes depleted of her own physical, emotional and spiritual reservoirs. Since her own needs have not been adequately met, she may resort to temporary fillers, such as food or alcohol.

The long-term effect of trying to be a female superhero is that she resents the objects of her crusades. Why? Because she eventually sees them as a burden. When she gets to the point that she ain't got no more super-charged batteries or kryptonite to keep her going, she resents people for coming to her. Even when she's so burned out and she's not able to give any more, she still feels bad about saying "no," so she resents anyone who puts her in the position of saying "no" and, she believes, makes her look weak.

She may also resent them because:

1. People no longer see her as human, but as a female superhero who always has her act together and is always there to help. Because of this, they no longer check in with her to see how things are going in her own world. So she feels they don't care about her unless she is focused on their needs.

2. No one gives her the same support she renders to others. A female superhero may have started her heroic crusade because she never had that support in the first place. Maybe she never even had love available to her when she needed it most. Maybe her parents or guardians had little to give her. She knows the pain of not having the support or love one needs, so she has vowed to always be there for others.

The problem is that because of her own emotional issues, her good intentions are driven by the wrong motive. "Maybe if I continually give myself to others, they might just do the same for me" are her sentiments. They fuel her actions as she pulls on her heroine outfit at the dawning of a new day.

To make matters worse, the female superhero may actually be misled into thinking that serving others in this manner is why she is here on earth. While she may be here to serve in some fashion, God may have intended for her to take another route or do things in a different manner – after all there are many ways to support people. However, her emotions are calling the shots, so she has not got time to think about what God wants.

Despite the fact that she is constantly servicing the needs of others, she is actually all about "me, me, me." And yet she doesn't know it. I can just see the horrified look on the female superhero's face if you were to point out that what she is doing is trying to get her own needs met in the wrong way.

THE FEMALE BULLY

The *female bully* thinks that being hard is the only way to get what she wants out of life. So she might come across as a ruthless, cutthroat, cruel, toe-treading tyrant of a woman in the business world — a force to be reckoned with, who can make some men quiver in their boots. For her, the notion of being emotional is out of the question. She has some masquerading tendencies, but her exterior is hard to crack. She may remain single because she holds to the idea that she doesn't need a man and wants to prove she can make her way through life on her own. That may easily be the case; but if you look deeper, you might find a woman who was hurt as a child, or even as an adult. In order to cope she has built a fortress around herself, so no one can come close, much less be allowed into her world.

The problem is that the same fortress gates that prevent people from coming in also prevent her from getting out. Like the masquerader, she often suffers from feelings of isolation that can be amplified by bouts of depression. However, because she believes her hard front has kept her going for such a long time, she assumes there is no other way than to be hard. What this woman needs is true love to help her build back her hope, trust and love for humanity.

THE FEMALE LOVE SEEKER

The *female love seeker* is a woman on a mission. Her mission is to find love and she will go to any lengths to get what she wants. Because of the intensity of her craving for love, she may end up satisfying this craving at a high cost to herself — such as paying for the love she seeks physically (by spending large amounts of money on her lover), sexually (by giving her body for sex in return for what she perceives is love), or emotionally (by participating in an abusive relationship) – if not all of the above. Though she is paying a high price for this "love," she accepts the unbalanced tradeoffs because she feels her need is being satisfied to some degree.

How did the female love seeker become this way? Well, she may have been starved for love from childhood, unable to have her needs met by her parents or guardians. Or it could be that the only love offered her was conditional. So she grew accustomed to paying a price to get love – such as being well behaved, making good grades or otherwise living up to others' expectations. The female love seeker may also have been a victim of abuse, which may have distorted her understanding of what true love is. This may have made her susceptible to bad relationships.

Whatever the early components were, the end product is that she makes her way through life paying dearly to get an inherent need met. If the female love seeker does not deal with this, the chances are that even when she is in good relationships where she feels genuine love and nothing is required of her, she may feel she needs to pay in some way. (This is not to be confused with the kind acts we all demonstrate to the ones we love. Instead, a female love seeker tends to go overboard, because she feels she is not worthy of the love and must make a payment.)

THE FEMALE HIDER

The *female hider* is hiding from love. This is not just the love from male-female relationships, but from relationships in general. Like the female bully, she has built up a strong fortress around her, disallowing people into her life or preventing her from coming out. This woman may be perceived by others as an extrovert. However, this outgoing style is more than likely a coping behaviour she has developed. Her aim is to be perceived as outgoing to stop people from getting closer to her. People may think they know her, but this is not true. The fact is that few, if any, people know who she really is, because she has been in hiding. She may also be the talkative type who continuously tries to keep the conversation going in the hope that it will never bring the focus back onto her.

Again, this woman has experienced such painful circumstances that her only way of dealing with them has been to retreat on the inside. The inside of her can be imagined as a deep cave, into which she travels deeper and deeper – away from the mouth of the cave, which is her gateway to the world. By retreating into the darkness of the cave, she believes that no one will be able to hurt her again.

The sad fact is that it also means others may never be able to reach out to her to pull her out of herself, much less to love her. The more pain the female hider experiences, the more deeply she retreats into the cave. Her hiding behaviour tends to bring along isolation and a deep aloneness. Over time, she learns to enjoy her own company, but she also longs to connect with people again. The only problem is that she is trapped so deeply in the cave that she cannot find her way back to the surface. She too must build her trust in people again and come back to the mouth of the cave into the arms of someone who loves her. This is where it takes the love of God and a supportive community to bring her back into fellowship with others.

To cope with her life in the depths of the cave, the female hider may end up daydreaming of better days or conjuring images in her mind that make her feel connected with others. She may resort to talking to herself or to others in her mind or even out loud. This helps her to cope with the isolation and the aloneness. She may develop other coping behaviours as long as it makes her feel her need for human connection is satisfied by other means.

The female hider wants to love and be loved, but does not know how to go about finding it. The chances are that she has been hurt, betrayed, rejected, abandoned or abused. Since then she has developed a contorted image of people and love. So trusting others is a problem for her.

However, this woman has probably learned to get on with her life. She may even be extremely successful. Remember, I said on the surface, it all looks great. She may end up remaining single – pushing away guys who genuinely love her — or she may end up married to a man who struggles to connect with her. If the man is not willing to provide enough support to pull her out of her cave, the marriage may ultimately break down.

THE FEMALE ATTENTION SEEKER

The *female attention seeker* is exactly what you would think – an attention seeker. This woman may not have had the love or attention of a parent — in particular, the one she may have been more fond of. She probably received little, if any, approval, affirmation and attention in her formative years for whatever reason. Maybe her parents/guardians were sparse with the praises and abundant with the criticism. Maybe none of her efforts were ever celebrated unless they were sheer perfection — getting an "A" or winning an award. She might have come in second place or attained "B's" instead. Whenever she did, she never quite gained the approval or affirmation of those she expected it from. She then internalised this rejection. And so she continues to strive for perfection. The woman who lives for this kind of attention keeps craving it even after reaching perfection status. A tendency for the female attention seeker is that she may only consider herself worthy or "good" when she achieves her goals.

So she may have grown up to be a workaholic or a perfectionist, trying to get affirmation, attention, praise, identity and fulfilment through her efforts, work, accomplishments, personality, apparel or whatever she owns. She is most likely convinced that if she does more, works harder or gives more of herself, she will get what she needs. So she sets high, if not impossible, goals and does everything within her power to accomplish them.

She may also exhibit negative behaviours, such as putting others down so she can look better than they do or using devious, cunning ways to fulfil her own agenda. At the sight of someone better than she is, she might just find herself in a tizzy, driven to competitive behaviour.

Another characteristic of the female attention seeker is that once she feels she has attained the attention she requires from someone or a particular project, the craving for her approval may suddenly disappear. But her craving for attention still remains as strong as ever. For example, maybe she has wanted the attention of a particular guy. As soon as he gives it to her, he may be surprised to find that she suddenly goes cold on him. Her need for attention still drives her, but now she's on to the next conquest to satisfy that craving. So she may come across as cold-hearted.

However, her tendencies are not limited to her personal life. I once knew a woman running her own business who would pour hundreds of hours and lots of money into trying to get new clients or secure contracts with huge organisations. As soon as they responded in a positive way – giving her the opportunity to pitch to the client or senior management, who had the power to award the contract — she lost interest. It was as if she had no desire to pursue the contract at all. All she wanted was to be acknowledged. Her satisfaction was in the fact that she got their attention.

Another dimension of the female attention seeker is she may not be able to accept compliments, no matter how genuine. When they are given, they may simply go over her head. She has not learned to internalise them. No wonder she remains driven. (However, this may be because of an underlying belief that people are dishonest or exaggerate. After all, she has spent her life doing tons of great things with no praise. So she may be sceptical. "Why now?" she may think to herself.)

By the way, if you come across a female attention seeker, you are probably looking at the face of a high achiever. The only problem is that she is not aware that she is one. She knows what her accomplishments are, of course. In fact, she can quote them with great acumen. But she does not *feel* successful. The assumption is that if she had really achieved as much as she is supposed to achieve, her hunger for approval and attention would subside. Since it doesn't, she assumes she is still not good enough yet. No matter what she achieved, she will probably never be convinced it is enough, unless she is healed from that which torments her.

THE FEMALE PESSIMIST

For the *female pessimist*, it is as if her hope in life has all but curled up and died. It's all doom and gloom. Nothing will ever work. Life is too hard. There are too many obstacles, so she cannot succeed.

Her destiny is out of her control. She has given up the fight. She does not think she stands any chance in accomplishing anything. No matter what opportunities she faces, they are seen as insurmountable.

I do not believe anyone comes out of the womb this way. Something must have happened to discourage her so deeply. Her history may have been marred with failure, abuse or even abandonment. Maybe there are things she once believed in, such as the institution of marriage, great relationships, a successful career or even the Christian faith. But somehow, she has felt let down, whether through a fault of her own or of others. So the fire that once kindled in her died a long time ago.

Unlike the female bully who hardens herself to life, hides her emotions and forcefully ploughs through life to get what she wants, the female pessimist doesn't try because she assumes that whatever she might aim for will not work. If she does take action, she expects it to fail. Therefore, her assumption of failure becomes a self-fulfilling prophecy and she does not accomplish a great deal. The idea of getting up to fight or taking her destiny into her own hands does not cross her mind. After all, she sees herself as being powerless to change anything at all. And so she, like her hope, curls up and dies inside, counting the days she has left in this hard and difficult world. If she had the courage to find a way out, especially when things get really tough, then I have no doubt she would opt out of the race of life, committing suicide.

THE FEMALE WEAKLING

The *female weakling* does not appear to have the strength to handle her life. She wears her heart on her sleeve, as an invitation to everyone to take advantage of her or trample on her. Yet she wonders why they do.

Not only does this kind of woman tend to feel as though life has treated her unfairly, this delicate soul feels sorry for herself. She may often find herself trapped in self-pity, asking, "Why me?" as she faces situations in her life. There may come a point where handling day-to-day life may be such a challenge that she may give up trying. Bouts of depression may be a regular thing for the female weakling through her consistent pity-parties and negative thoughts.

The female weakling does not expect good things to happen to her. When genuine people actually do nice things, she often feels they have a hidden agenda. Yet she may also want to express her gratitude over and beyond what is necessary or latch on to them. Because of this, she might end up chasing people away. Her low self-esteem means the female weakling is a magnet for trouble. She seems to attract the wrong kind of relationships out of her own neediness. The female weakling's relationships may be one-sided because of her lack of boundaries. She may move from one abusive relationship to another and wonder why people keep being so horrible to her. Her poor boundaries mean she does not defend her territory well. Standing up for herself may be a big issue for her. If only she realised that it is her God-given right to stand up for herself as His precious daughter. The sad fact is that this woman may never know how special she really is.

❧

What all of these female hybrids need is an internal adjustment of the spiritual, mental and emotional kind. Whichever way you look at it, female hybrids are a poor reflection of the awesome women God has created. Because of the unresolved emotional issues they are carrying, we cannot see their authentic selves. This means that the world never gets to experience, enjoy and celebrate the amazing women they are.

Moreover, as we continue to sprint our way through life, we simply don't get a chance to reflect on ourselves and correct or even eliminate anything that may be moulding us into someone we are not or forcing us to develop female hybrid tendencies. Our busy lifestyles mean that we infrequently pause to see what's driving us to do the things we do. This has a detrimental effect on us.

Therefore, over the course of this book, we will be spending some time getting an understanding of the true woman God had in mind. For the time being, please bear in mind that none of these female hybrid tendencies is God's desire for you. They are a vague, if not poor, resemblance of the women God had in mind.

JOURNALING MOMENT
Which Type Are You?

Sister, I would like you to spend some time reflecting on the above female hybrid types. Do any of these resemble you? Maybe you see yourself in a number of the different categories as some of the traits overlap. Or maybe your type is not listed. Either way, take some time out to jot down some traits you have recognised in your life. For each trait, try to identify what has been the motivating factor or what has driven you to that particular trait.

_____

_____

_____

_____

_____

_____

_____

_____

Chapter Five

Emotional Baggage Of The Female Hybrid

*I*n my time working with women for the past decade as a coach and consultant, not only have I been able to identify emerging patterns of behaviours of the female hybrid, I discovered that a number of female hybrids, if not all of them, were carrying a lot of excess baggage as they journeyed through life. The content of their emotional baggage turned out to be the driving force of their attitudes, beliefs and behaviours.

I have no doubt that some, if not all, of these issues can be observed not just in women, but in men as well. Having worked with a number of male corporate professionals, particularly those in leadership roles, I tend to believe this is true. However, since this book is directed primarily to women, we will focus our attention on women's needs and issues.

Below is my top ten list of the emotional issues that are the major causes of emotional imbalance in women's lives. Let's take a peek into the dainty handbag of the modern female hybrid to see what these emotional accessories contain.

Issue 1: Unresolved Problems, Past Or Present

Unresolved problems could come from painful experiences in the past or present such as physical abuse, sexual abuse, a troubled or failed relationship or a work-related problem. What I have noticed is that when unresolved problems occur, we tend to add them to our pile – hence we end up accumulating a lot of baggage.

Let's take a peek into the dainty handbag of the modern female hybrid to see what these emotional accessories contain.

Now, whether we like it or not, bad stuff *will* happen. It's just a fact of life. However, it's how you choose to deal with it that matters. And believe me, these things must be dealt with, because their impact can be astounding. From my personal experience, as well as that of a number of women I have worked with, I can say that unresolved problems have a powerful effect in hampering people's lives.

One particular business owner I've spoken to had been the victim of sexual abuse as a child and had been carrying her baggage for years without dealing with it. No one was aware of the fact that her way of dealing with it included finding comfort in food and crying fits. As she had not dealt with the problem, she had resented men for a number of years and had developed domineering tendencies, since she never wanted to be overpowered by another man again. Unknown to her, it affected the way she ran her business, her relationships and much more. Thankfully, with support, she was able to overcome the years of resentment, lack of forgiveness, guilt and shame, so she could move on with her life. Once she was free from the heavy weight of her baggage, she was able to start making the right decisions for her life and her business. One of the things she observed was that she felt freer and did not have to turn to food to receive comfort.

Issue 2: Low Self-Esteem

Self-esteem generally refers to how we feel about or value ourselves. So if you have low self-esteem, you may lack self-respect and self-worth. For someone in this predicament, I would suggest getting into God's Word to see what He thinks and says about you versus what you have come to believe.

I have lost track of the number of women I have come across or worked with who have been bitten by this bug. It's amazing because all of them without exception were amazing women and had a lot going for themselves in various aspects of their lives. However, they could not see it. Somewhere down the line, they had come to build an inaccurate impression of themselves based on the external influences I've been referring to — the media, culture, religion, family, friends and much more. This then manifests itself in a million ways, such as hooking up with the wrong guy who spots their low self-esteem a mile away and takes advantage of them. And they tolerate it.

I have known an entrepreneur who placed so little value on herself and her products and services that it was reflected in the way she presented herself, ran her business and even priced her products and services. She devalued her offerings by making them cheaper than they ought to have been, by not placing enough value on them. In actual fact, they were worth their weight in gold.

We see this happening frequently in the corporate world too as many potential highfliers short-change themselves because of their own negative self-beliefs. If it is not dealt with, low self-esteem can keep you from reaching success and can fill your life with unhappiness in your career, relationships and much more. When I work with these individuals, I spend a lot of time helping them change their self-beliefs to healthier ones. Over time they become free from low self-esteem and start soaring in various aspects of their lives.

Issue 3: Poor Personal Boundaries

This is an issue that women often don't want to own up to. In some cases, they are simply ignorant of the fact that they are living a boundary-less life.

Women with poor personal boundaries tend to find themselves saying "yes" when they want to say "no." Like the female superhero, they may be overwhelmed with guilt when they do say "no" and may even agree to do things they don't want to do because they can't stand to say "no." They also lack the ability to tell people what behaviours are acceptable towards them and the consequences they might face if they breach these boundaries. In part, they fear the repercussions of doing so.

Please bear in mind that healthy boundaries are within our God-given rights as His children. God Himself set copious boundaries in the Bible. Otherwise, how would we know when we crossed the line? Moreover, God never says "yes" if He means to say "no". So if we use God for a model, as we should, we have every right to do the same.

One client of mine was a female professional who could not say "no" to other people's demands for her money and her time. Because of her lack of boundaries, she never had enough time to spend on the things she wanted to do such as her own personal aspirations, as there were constant cries for help from those around her. The people all around her also saw her as their local ATM or bank and she was forever giving away what amounted to huge sums of money. I can hear my Christian Sisters asking, "What's wrong with that? After all, that's the Christian thing to do." Let me just say a few things about that, despite the Scriptures about generosity and giving you can easily quote for me.

God has given each and every one of us the responsibility to live our lives. For example, it is my responsibility to work, manage my finances, use my time effectively, nurture and develop my being, build my relationship with God and others – and a whole lot more. God did not intend me to carry your load or compensate for your lack of responsibility. The moment I start to do that, I become burdened with more than what God designed for me to carry. This will have a detrimental impact on me in the long run. I cannot live your life for you or regularly compensate for your failure to handle being an adult. That's your responsibility and you have to be ready to suffer the consequences if you do not handle it well.

ଔ

God has given each and every one of us the responsibility to live our lives.

ଔ

Didn't the Bible say, "He who does not work should not eat"? The same could go for those who work but choose to spend their money frivolously. If you choose to use your pay checks to buy the latest designer pieces and have no money to pay your rent, that's your business, not mine. This may sound harsh and lacking in compassion, but how else would the other person learn?

Now there are always exceptions to this, such as when a person has experienced a personal setback of some sort. We are called to support each other and carry each other's burdens; but burdens don't last for eternity. It would have been foolish for the man rescued by the Good Samaritan to expect the Samaritan to take care of him for the rest of his life (Luke 10:30-37). The Samaritan played his part till the man was able to get back on his feet and get on with life. This is a clear model for us to follow.

The problem the boundary-less person has is that she continues to support the other person long after the necessity has passed, or she is unclear what her responsibilities are – to herself and to others. Hence such people keep giving till it starts to impact their lives. Didn't the Bible say, "Love thy neighbour as thyself"? This means I ought to do for my neighbours what I would do for myself.

The problem is that some do for their neighbours and don't do for themselves. I see this happening time and time again. When I support clients in managing their finances better, the first thing that is obvious is what they give to others. However, they don't do the same for themselves. So the chances are they have no long-term savings plan and no emergency fund. Their current accounts are a mess and they have put important plans or goals on hold as a result. I have yet to find one such individual who can get the same financial help from the people she has been pouring out support for. While I am an advocate of sowing and reaping, I let God direct my steps in whom to give to and what to give. I believe there is a moral to the story here.

The secret is to say "yes" from your heart and "no" from your head. What I mean is, feel for people from your heart, but think through your decisions before you go out there to save the world. Make sure your reservoirs are full as you pour things out. Moreover, deal with your own issues by creating new boundaries or rules for your life.

For some, your issue may not be with money, but it may be an overbearing boss, a parent or relative who treats you as a child, or a partner who abuses you. Whatever it is, don't tolerate it anymore. Let them know what the consequences of their actions will be.

Issue 4: Unmet Personal Needs

As humans, we all have personal needs that make us feel more like ourselves when they are met. Unmet needs come about through gaps that have occurred in our development. Examples of these include the need to be accepted, recognised, affirmed, loved, encouraged, heard and so on. There is a tendency for us not to get all our needs met or to get enough of it.

If our personal needs aren't met, it tends to slow down our development and diminish the quality of our lives. In the continued absence of our real needs being met, we may find other means to replace what we really need to keep us going (e.g. food, work, sex, drugs, etc.). This is the reason some of us reach for food or throw ourselves into our work when our innate personal needs are deficient. However, food, work and so on are not the answer.

I have been there when it comes to seeking comfort from food. That's why they call it "comfort food." Imagine seeking comfort from a tub of ice cream or a bar of chocolate. But isn't that what we do? In the times we feel isolated, stressed or in despair, we head for food. Yes, we may get temporary comfort, but it does not last. Hence we keep giving ourselves a food fix. Over the years, my food fix did nothing to meet my needs. Instead, it had an impact on my wardrobe!

Another popular unmet need I've come across is the need for recognition and affirmation. It's not that people want to be put on a pedestal and have others sing their praises. It's that human thing in us that makes us want people to acknowledge us as individuals and notice our achievements. We are all born with varying degrees of this inherent need. Have you noticed how children tend to call for the attention of their parents when they feel they have excelled at something? They tend to say "Look at me" or Look at what I have done". What do you suppose is going on there? They are seeking for recognition, praise and feedback.

We all have the need to feel appreciated and valued. It inspires us to do even more. The trap we fall into is that, if we do not feel like we are getting these needs met, we work harder, longer hours and may even go to great lengths or use dubious means to get what we want.

I am sure you have a story or two to tell about people you have had the unfortunate experience of working with who were driven by this need. I have seen people put themselves under alarming pressures to accomplish what they feel would meet this need. In the end, it becomes a vicious circle. I encourage you to find a healthier way of getting this need met. For example, if you have endeavoured to get this need met at work, try to find a non-work environment where you can get this met (e.g., a competitive sport). It's much better than becoming a workaholic, ruining relationships and much more.

Issue 5: Lack Of Self-Confidence

A woman who lacks self-confidence or has insecurities doesn't trust in her own abilities, decisions and judgement. This may result in her not having the confidence to attempt something she is actually capable of accomplishing. An insecure woman may feel threatened when she perceives she is around someone who is better than she is, because she doubts herself. Consequently, she may act out of character through the use of negative emotions and behaviours.

If you feel insecure, you need to recognise that there will *always* be someone better than you at whatever activity or skill you're comparing. So get over it! Instead, look at the unique set of attributes you bring to the table. After all, our unique journeys in life make us who we are. And since we have not travelled the same road, we all have something unique to offer. Just like the woman with low self-esteem, you need to re-program your mind with God's Word. Also, you would benefit from developing a healthy self-awareness.

You may want to start out by listing all the good things about yourself — your strengths, abilities and successes — and meditate on these for a little while. We often lose sight of these as we hurriedly make our way through life; or we see them as not important, while admiring the apparently greener grass on the other side of the fence.

I remember working with a highly intelligent corporate professional who had a list of skills and qualifications a mile long, but she was not getting jobs that matched them. When we probed deeper, I found that she had a hard time seeing her assets. She could not envision herself with a better job, despite all she was bringing to the table. I tell you, this woman would have been an asset to any organisation, but she failed to see this. So we started working on improving her self-confidence, working through some of her fears and strengthening her personal foundation. Needless to say, over a period of time, she started attracting jobs suited to her, until she finally landed the job of her dreams. I know for sure we have not heard the last of this amazing woman who found her self-confidence.

Issue 6: Loss Of Unique Identity

As you can see from my recognition of female hybrids in our culture, I believe there are far too many women living as replicas of other people today. A large number of women seem to be obsessed with the idea of being like certain prominent figures, especially the ones they see on TV or on the pages of magazines. They want the body, weight, attitude, beliefs and successes of these people, even though they know so little about them. While it is great to have godly role models you can learn from, your aspirations should not include becoming a replica of another person. She has been created to be who she is and you have been created to be who you are. None of us was created to be a replica of, not pf someone else. Look for positive attitudes and behaviours in others to emulate, but do not try to model yourself to be someone you aren't.

Some women spend their whole lives listening to external voices that dictate to them who they should be, what they should do, wear, eat, look like and much more. Women who do this are literally dancing to the tunes of others, with few or none of their own rules to govern their own lives. After a period of time, they are no longer aware of who they really are.

I have found this to be consistent with people who have been caught up in the rat race, who have spent their lives pursuing other people's dreams, or have placed their own desires and uniqueness on hold for far too long. As I mentioned earlier, I have stopped this kind of woman to answer simple questions, such as, "Who are you?" "What do you like and dislike?" "What motivates you?" "What are your own personal values?" "If you had an opportunity to do something you have always wanted to do, what would that be?" Time and again, I've found that they are not able to come up with an answer!

I realise that some of these questions require a lot of thought. If I were to ask you what your purpose was in life, you may take a moment to answer, as well. However, your values, beliefs, likes and dislikes and motivators are what make you who you are. If you don't know the answers to these questions, you may be holding onto the beliefs, values and preferences of someone else.

I believe we should each stand for something, or we'll end up standing for everything – which is not ideal, because what you stand for makes you unique. Above all, when you embrace the notions of others, you will find that over time, you become dissatisfied, disquieted and unhappy with your life. This is one of the top reasons individuals come to me as a coach and consultant. And I love seeing their progress over time as they retrace their steps back to discovering who they are and creating new rules for their lives. The end result is fulfilment, internal joy and a meaningful life.

Years ago, I worked at a well-known global corporation. I had a particular career aspiration, which I knew I could achieve within this organisation. But I found I was continually opposed by managers who kept saying I could not do *XYZ* until I did *ABC* for a certain period of time. And even if I did *ABC*, there was no guarantee that I would reach my ambitions, simply because they said so. They wanted me to become a clone.

I don't think they realised they had a nonconformist on their hands who would not take "no" for an answer and would never roll over and play dead. Unknown to them, I'd had an inspiring conversation with the CEO of the corporation before I had accepted the job. To me, he was a great man of vision and was the epitome of success and leadership in one body. He said some things that propelled me to where I am today. He was supportive of individuality, creativity and much more. And yet I was battling with his senior managers and one of his directors to be allowed to express the very individuality and creativity he encouraged. The director's parting statement to me was, "If you don't like things the way they are and will not do as I say, you can leave!"

I did leave, all right; but not until I had proved him wrong. Despite his predictions, I reached my personal aspirations within months (not years!) and gained the valuable experience that propelled me to greater heights. Sister, I thank God for His support, courage and strength during this time when I was facing my Goliath. I was anxious during the battle, but I realised I had to fight for my own uniqueness. I refused to become a faceless, voiceless clone in a huge corporation. This experience alone fuelled me to write a series of the programs I teach women. It will come as no surprise to you that one of them was called "Will the Real Me Please Stand Up!"

There are far too many conforming, un-opinionated employees already. Sadly, many often fail to leave an impression, leave a legacy or make a difference. I am in no way suggesting anarchy. But I do encourage you to stand up and be counted through your unique identity.

When people become replicas, they force into the background the very person they were created to be and replace it with what they have picked up externally. I suggest you press the pause button and do not release it till you have rediscovered the real you. Answer questions like:

> What am I like?
> What do I like and don't I like?
> What attributes, skills and talents do I have to offer?
> What are my strengths and areas of limitation?
> What are my personal values and personal needs?
> What motivates me?
> What do I want out of my life?

You may find value in posing these questions to those nearest and dearest to you. Ask them what they think of you in answer to these questions. You may benefit from carrying out a personalised 360° feedback by asking your boss, peers and direct reports to help you identify more about yourself. After all, we all have blind spots. It's only when you start to do this that you begin to gain clarity on the great woman God created you to be.

Issue 7: Personal Value Deficiency

We all have personal values we live by that go beyond family, morality, religion, tradition or culture. Values form a part of us and can be described as things we are naturally drawn to or disposed to do with little or no effort. These include the following: impacting, inspiring, creating, excelling, nurturing, accomplishing and much more. When a person ignores her own values, she may find herself frustrated and unfulfilled within herself until she starts honouring her values.

Therefore, the onus is on you to find out what your personal values are. Holding onto other people's values will surely bring you misery. You might begin by asking yourself, "What do I have a natural ability to do? What can I do with little or no effort? What appeals to me naturally?"

I remember how I felt in some of my previous careers when my values where not being honoured. It frustrated me. Each day I spent at work felt like I was in a bath with my socks on. It did not feel right, regardless of what the job entailed. And I seemed to be getting the Monday-morning blues every day!

It was after a few frustrating career choices that I decided to take time out to focus on identifying my personal values. Needless to say, because I did this you are now holding the results of one of my values in your hand! It is my value to inspire people through writing – something I had had a secret passion to do for years. Honestly speaking, I have not looked back since. I know I can say the same for heaps of my clients who not only discovered what their values were but got on track to living them. From speaking to them, I know they are much happier.

Issue 8: Spiritual Apathy

In our search for success and all its trappings, I have observed that many have forsaken or shown a lack of concern for developing their spirits. Matters have not been helped by organisations and schools throwing out Christian values, concepts and activities so as to appear to be more liberal. The result of this includes an undeveloped and poorly nurtured spirit. This in turn gives rise to the lopsided adult I referred to earlier, the female hybrid.

An important fact to bear in mind is that our spirits are an essential part of our beings. They must not be neglected, as they are the glue that holds together our bodies and souls. Our spirits are our way of connecting with God. By being in tune with your spirit, you become aware of things such as your higher calling or purpose. Therefore, if you have not connected with God or have backslidden, I encourage you to get connected.

When I jumped on the success bandwagon, I made the mistake of leaving behind my spirit as I raced through life. Big mistake! I later realised that my greatest accomplishments had taken place only when I stayed connected with the One who had sent me here in the first place. When you are connected online, you can surf the Net, check your email and do a whole raft of things, but when you are disconnected, you are isolated from a great deal of things. It's the same way with the spirit. The trick is to remain connected.

Issue 9: Inadequate Self-Investment

From my experience, I find this to be a characteristic trait of those who care for others, who have a supportive profession, who have huge amounts of responsibility or who are high achievers. Because of their roles, they expend a great deal of energy accomplishing their tasks. However, the problem arises when they fail to refill their own reservoirs until they are depleted of resources to keep them going.

In addition to this, a number of women tend not to have adequate support mechanisms in place so they can continue to be effective in their roles. They fail to grasp that they can only give what they have.

It's like planning a long-distance trip in your car. Because of your urgency to get there, you fail to do the necessary maintenance tasks for your car, such as checking the oil levels, servicing the car or filling it with fuel. Imagine embarking on the trip with a tank half-empty and not stopping for a refill. Imagine not taking breaks or making stopovers to rest and recharge yourself. How far would you expect to get?

Yet isn't that what so many of us do, thinking we are female superheroes who can keep going and going and going? Our favourite saying becomes, "We have not got the time for this!" and we skip over our most essential activities.

As much as I find this trait in the secular world, I have found it equally among my Christian brethren and myself. We seem to think we have to continually be on the go, pouring ourselves into the lives of others and never investing in our own lives.

It's true that the Bible does encourage us to use what God has placed in our hands to serve others. After all, that was one of the things Jesus came to demonstrate to us. However, Jesus demonstrated wisdom by knowing when to retreat from the crowds (the equivalent of our roles and responsibilities). He knew when to simply stop pouring out, chill out with His friends or spend time with God. He also had a supportive system of disciples He could open up to and rely on for support. So my question is this: If Jesus, the greatest Leader in history, can find the time to do this, why can't you?

The long-term result for people without adequate self-investment is that they inevitably burn out. They may also flip out one day and go over the top on self-indulgence. They may also begin to resent their role or responsibilities.

Therefore, the moral to the story is that we are to live a balanced life of pouring in and pouring out. After all, you are the main benefactor of all this. Often when I got myself into this frazzle, my mum used to remind me of the fact that if I wanted to live long enough to enjoy the fruits of my labours, I had better slow down. My mum's great advice has saved me from many enormous despairs.

Issue 10: Losing Touch With Yourself

This is another modern syndrome among super-busy women, both in the secular world and in the church. You lose touch with yourself when you get so busy or preoccupied that you can't see what's going on within you and beyond as you are juggling too many things in your mind.

Let me ask you this: Do you ever get so busy that you forget important things? Do you leave one room in your house and go to another to get something and you can't remember why you are there?

Or maybe you leave your house to go somewhere and you can't remember why. Do you seem to be losing things because you absent-mindedly left them somewhere else?

These examples may seem trivial, but are they really? Is it because we have gotten preoccupied with the big things that we have come to trivialise some everyday activities? It makes me wonder if we are enjoying our journey at all when we are missing out on the details of our lives.

I have just highlighted some of the external things that can happen, but losing touch with yourself is not just about external things. My question is, if you have lost focus on the *external* things relating to you, what about the *internal* things relating to you?

When last did you check in with the emotional baggage you may have accumulated of late? We all go through things every day of our lives and can accumulate bad stuff along the way. When last did you check up on your state of mind, emotions or spirit? When it comes to your body or your car, you get things checked out. But what about the rest of you? The other things are equally important.

So my argument is that to attain an abundant, successful life of meaning requires that you not only focus on your goals and aspirations, but on all aspects of your life!

I know the pace of life nowadays rarely gives us permission to slow down and check in with ourselves, but do it anyway! If not, the result is that, over a period of time, you can become detached from your real self. What you then find is that you lack a healthy of awareness of the true condition of your being. Oblivious to this, you open yourself up to the likelihood of facing long-term detrimental problems with your spirit, soul and body.

‪‪‪

Did you spot any of your own emotional issues in my top ten list? Coach Gladys says, "Overcome them"!

Just a little reminder: None of these issues is God's best for your life. So what I am saying is that you do not have to remain the way you are or settle for carrying this stuff around with you. Correctly identify the things that are going on within you and take steps to overcome them.

PART 3

Survival Techniques Of The Female Hybrid

Chapter Six

Coping Behaviours Of The Female Hybrid

OK, so you may have identified that you have evolved into a *female hybrid*. But you keep arguing that it's not a problem, since you have been doing well all this time! After all, you have made it in certain areas of your life, right? I hear you loud and clear! I also had some difficulty in reconciling the fact that one could be accomplishing great things yet still belong to the female hybrid clan.

Personally, I believe this is due to the way God made us. We have the ability to cope and to adapt ourselves to everyday life. This in itself is an essential life skill, as it would be detrimental to us if we fell to bits each time change occurred. But there is change and there is *change!*

What I mean is that there is change that involves things like relocating, getting married, having a child, losing a job, dealing with a broken friendship and so on. On the other end of the scale are situations such as the loss of a child, the diagnosis of a terminal illness, the trauma of rape or the experience of divorce. These are major changes, if not huge burdens. However, the point is that all change requires us to cope and adapt – something we have an ability to do as humans. All you need to do is glance through the Bible to see how people have adapted to their changing worlds. Ruth is a prime example of coping and adapting through the change of losing her husband at a young age.

Don't we simply adjust ourselves to the weight we carry by using certain parts of our being to balance the load, so we too can make the things we accomplish look like they are effortless?

So a woman could be accomplishing great things, yet still be a hybrid. This brings my thoughts to vivid images of the street hawkers I saw as a child in Nigeria. These were street traders or sellers who sold their goods by roaming from street to street carrying their merchandise on their heads. I was always fascinated by these hawkers, who would carry huge loads on their heads – hands free! I often wondered how they were able to carry these huge loads, let alone balance them without buckling under them or tipping them over.

After trying it myself a several times, I learned quickly that there was a knack to it. First, you needed a cloth rolled up into a tight circle that would act as a buffer between you and the load. Let's call it your "buffering cloth." Second, you needed to shift yourself under the load — through the use of your head, neck and body — ensuring that the load was balanced at all times. When I did that, I found that, all of a sudden, I was doing it — carrying a great load on top of my head, while making it look effortless. Aha! The penny finally dropped for me.

76

Isn't this what we do with the huge emotional baggage we carry day in and day out? Don't we simply adjust ourselves to the weight we carry by using certain parts of our being to balance the load, so we too can make the things we accomplish look like they are effortless? What we don't realise is that, just as the street hawker is making huge demands on certain muscle groups, so we are making huge demands on our tripartite beings – more than we were designed to carry on a daily basis. It's no surprise that many people are buckling under their own loads, are tripped up by them and even opt out of the race of life.

And as for our buffering cloth, though teeny in size in comparison to the load we carry, it is whatever we choose to use to protect us from the potentially sharp pain of the loads. Your cloth may be food (or the lack of it). For others, it could be drugs, alcohol, sex or any other addictive, compulsive or impulsive behaviour.

JOURNALING MOMENT

What's Your Buffer?

Sister, I consider this a fantastic opportunity to hit the pause button and just reflect on some of the things we have been talking about. What buffers have you put in place to support you in carrying the load you have been carrying? You might want to take a trip down memory lane and see how you have coped during certain moments of your life. Consider the impact of the buffers on your life today.

_____

_____

_____

_____

_____

_____

For me, one of the buffers I used was crying. I have lost count of the untold number of crying sessions that took place behind the scenes. That was the only way I knew to balance the load I was carrying. And boy, was there a lot of weeping in the night seasons! But you know what, Sis? Somehow I always managed to muster enough strength to face yet another day.

Once the curtains were raised, I gave yet another great performance! But when they came down, I was brought face to face with my feelings once again. The real problem was that my emotional issues were getting me down and I seemed powerless to do anything about them. Sure enough, after a number of great, but exhausting, performances, I found it more and more difficult to perform.

I chose to use the word *perform* to help you picture an actor or actress coming out on stage to act out a part, because that's what a number of us do day in, day out. We spend our lives rehearsing our lines and putting a lot of effort into looking the part. Therefore, make-up and clothing become part of our masquerading tools, as well as enhancing our outward appearance. Then the curtain rises and we do our thing.

But there is only one problem with performing. Life is not one big play that we are rehearsing for or performing in. It's the real thing! You only have one shot at it. I've learned to tell myself this fact time and time again in order to keep focused and grounded. The authentic women we have been created to be require that the real you and me show up at all times — without masks, of course!

Maybe you think performing isn't such a bad idea since, on the surface, you seem to be doing well for yourself and it's benefiting others. I used to share this thought too until I realized I was not the complete and balanced woman God had in mind when He delicately put me together. I had far too much emotional baggage that I was dragging along with me onto the stages of life. In the long run, your baggage limits your personal effectiveness. Also, you can only stretch so far before you grind to a halt. The weight of it will burn you out.

Have you ever tried running a marathon with a backpack containing huge rocks strapped to you? You wouldn't get far before you ran out of energy. Eventually, your muscles would give up once they were worked to their limit. This was the state in which I found myself at times. It was how I lived for a number of years till I woke up.

I woke up to the fact that my sole focus had been on performing. I had sprinted through life while burying a number of issues in the recesses of my mind, thinking they would be safe there. But guess what? When the trials of life came by, they rose to the surface. It was during these times that I often felt powerless as my issues stared me right in the face. I did not know what to do with them.

If it were a financial challenge or career situation, I could handle it with my typical two-pronged approach, which was to do what I could do and then leave the whole matter safely in God's capable hands. But what was this high flyer supposed to do with matters of the heart? In such matters, nothing I did improved the situation. As a matter of fact, any strategy I put in place worsened my condition, such as comfort eating (I gained weight), shutting myself away from the crowd (isolation) and much more. These things never really solved the problems at hand. Therefore, I had this overwhelming feeling of powerlessness. That was almost unheard of in my world.

With the little energy I had, all I could do was talk to Father about what I was facing. After all, things were now proving way too big for little me to handle. But I had grown tired of pretending, like those around me, that everything was OK. I knew I was not living the fullness of life God had promised me, so something had to change. I refused to go on with my life this way. This was the beginning of my personal journey to emotional wholeness.

Have you been like I was, performing on the stages of life, only to have to deal with your own emotional issues when the curtains come down? Have you acknowledged that you have unknowingly joined the female hybrid clan? Is your emotional life akin to a roller coaster, peaking and dipping, as you go through different seasons in your life? One day you are fine, yet the next your whole world seems to be falling apart, triggered by certain situations. Are you prone to having your emotions dictate your actions? Do you feel on some days that you are making progress and you are so over your emotional baggage, then other days, they overwhelm you all over again? Do you find yourself falling into the same patterns time and time again despite the numerous promises you make to yourself and to God? Or maybe you are just hurting all the time, hoping that someday it will all be over?

Sister, your emotional well-being is something you cannot afford to ignore any longer.

Sister, this is the time to be real. After all, it's between you, this book and God – no one else! It's not so much that you have not recognized what's going on in your emotional life. The real problem is that you are powerless to do anything about it — in your own strength, that is.

Hopefully by now you are recognising that this is not God's best for you. It's not His plan for you to be emotionally high one day and low the next. How could anyone live her life in such a state, let alone fulfil her purpose in life? It's practically impossible to give your best to anything in this condition. We all have a purpose here on planet earth. If you want to effectively utilize your natural gifts to make a difference, it requires wholeness in every facet of your life, regardless of who you are or what your status is. How can you expect to accomplish this successfully with holes in your foundation?

In order for you to continue to do all the great stuff you do and to make an impact in life, some essential foundational work will have to be done. This is even more crucial if you are leading or managing others; are in an influential position at home, at church or in a corporation; or you are determined to live a successful and purposeful life. Sister, your emotional well-being is something you cannot afford to ignore any longer. Continuing to hide or ignore your issues will cripple you and may even hinder, pervert or make you forfeit your future altogether.

My intention is to support you in becoming the emotionally balanced woman you were created to be. However, if you're still thinking this is a load of fluffy stuff, touchy-feely spiritual mumbo jumbo, you might do well to remember one thing: You are a tripartite being consisting of spirit, soul and body. These three areas need to be fully functional at all times in order for you to succeed in life and fulfil your purpose.

Have you ever stopped to consider why some people soar to glory and then fall to shame? What do you suppose was going on there? Could it be that some essential foundational work was missing that should have been dealt with in their waiting room days? Who knows? We read about so many spiritual and secular giants who rise to greatness, but never complete their purpose. If we are to learn from others, it makes sense that you and I pay close attention to our spirit, soul and body, too. They all need nourishment and need to be developed. Don't make the mistake of overlooking one for the other. Big mistake! Think about it. It's like putting an effort into dressing up your body with trendy clothing, yet abusing it with extreme stress, long hours on the job, alcohol abuse, smoking and unhealthy eating habits. Sounds foolish, but isn't that what we do?

Remember, just because you appear to be successful in other areas of your life doesn't mean you can overlook your emotional well-being or that your soul is in mint condition. Think about the female hybrid traits. A number of female hybrids I have met were not unsuccessful or low achievers. They were influential and prosperous, to say the least. But as anyone honest enough would tell you, the downside of this kind of life is that your emotional baggage will weigh you down and pull you in different directions. The end result is that it has a tendency to nullify your "good intentions and faithful deeds" as the Bible says in Second Thessalonians 1:11. So I guess your aim ought to be to put an equal amount of effort into dealing with and strengthening this crucial part of your being rather than overlooking it.

Chapter Seven

Looking For Restoration
In The Wrong Places

I think it is safe to say that at one time or another, many of us have looked for solutions to eliminate the effects of our emotional baggage — in all the wrong places.

We have seen how our female hybrid tendencies drive our behaviours and emotions. We have learned that we also develop coping behaviours to buffer the heavy load we carry around with us. Our fast-paced, high-flying lifestyles don't help matters either, as they afford us little or no time to pause and reflect, let alone nourish our tripartite beings. The deceptive traps so prevalent in our modern society, where anything goes, have only compounded the problem. Whatever feels right, looks good or is of popular opinion tends to be the determining factor of the method we choose to deal with the issues in our lives.

The result of this is that we have simply added fuel to the fires already raging in our lives. You wouldn't try to put out a fire by dousing it with petrol, would you? But that's exactly what we are doing! Our precarious methods have opened a can of worms, made matters worse and ended up pushing people in the wrong direction — further away from God. This means more and more people plunge further into despair.

You wouldn't try to put out a fire by dousing it with petrol, would you? But that's exactly what we are doing!

Sister, have you experienced the empty promises of a bottle of alcohol, a drug, a food binge or sexual immorality? You may experience a short-lived euphoria; but notice how you have to keep going back to it whenever you are having one of your moments? Before you know it, you have a new emotional issue to add to your list – an addiction.

Without jumping ahead of myself, I want us to take a peek into the lives of some women, Sisters like you and me, who have faced such real-life issues. Let's see how they have tried to calm the raging seas in their lives. Who knows? You may be able to relate to one or more of them.

DRINKING HER SORROWS AWAY

Roberta never thought she would end up as one of those who drank their sorrows away. She had always seen those types of people as weak, with little or no self-control, as they allowed the poison to slowly wreck their lives. But then one day, she found herself in the same boat.

"How did I end up here?" she thought as she clumsily poured out the last few drops of the alcohol into her glass. "Oh, what the heck!" she blurted out loud, holding the bottle close to her chest. After all, her newly found friend, alcohol, made her feel good. It kept her from having to deal with the fact that Michael, her husband of thirteen years, had walked out on her. With the alcohol, she could just about remain on this side of sanity. It calmed her nerves.

Coming home to an empty house always seemed to drive a knife into her heart, as the painful memories of the night Michael left flooded her mind. After all, this was their home; they had built it together. They had spent many nights in front of the fireplace with a bottle of wine, sharing their plans and dreams for the rest of their lives. Now here she was in front of the fireplace...alone with an empty bottle. Feeling helpless, she grabbed yet another bottle and poured yet another drink. It had been a long time since the alarm bells had rung in her head about the amount she was consuming.

As she brought the glass to her mouth, streams of tears rolled down her face. "God, why does it hurt so much?"

Roberta felt so lonely. It had been six weeks, four days and eight hours since Michael had broken the news to her. If you had asked her, she would have told you that she had a good thing going in her marriage. Then he told her that he had made a mistake in marrying her. He also went on to say he had been unhappy until recently, when he had found another woman, whom he believed to be his true soul mate.

"Can you believe that?" Roberta muttered to the bottle in her hand. "I gave thirteen years of my life to that man. He told me he loved me. What do I do now?"

This was not how she had imagined her marriage to turn out. Yet here she was: hurt, confused and afraid to talk about her aching heart. Another glass of wine looked more appealing than ever.

It was a frightening thought to be single again. She was already in her mid-fifties. Lord knows it had taken her long enough to find a man in the first place. She could not bear the thought of rejoining the other hordes of single sisters, all sitting pretty and waiting for Mr.

Right. The only difference was that she had no intention of allowing a man into her life again. As she mulled over what she might have done wrong, more and more glasses of wine disappeared, until yet another bottle was empty.

This became Roberta's routine after she came home from work. What was only supposed to be a social drink to calm her nerves and relieve some of her pain became an addiction she had not bargained for. Roberta soon recognized that she had a bigger problem on her hands than just her broken marriage. She was routinely picking herself up off of her front room floor in the morning with no recollection of the night before. Roberta's broken marriage had opened doors to a lot more than she had bargained for. She had a dependency on alcohol – an old habit she had beaten over ten years before.

YOU ARE NOT WHAT YOU WEIGH

Patricia was a beautiful 34-year-old woman who had so much going for her. By the time she was thirty, she had accomplished what many women twice her age could only dream of. She was a high-flying attorney in one of the world's top five law firms. She owned a string of sports cars, lived in a penthouse in the best part of town, and owned both a summer home on an exclusive island and a winter home in a posh ski resort. Not only that, she owned a string of properties around the world. She mingled with high-powered people and had a track record of winning all her cases. To top it all off, she wore designer labels and had an enviable figure to go with it. Patricia's life would have been great had it not been marred with a dark secret. She had a huge problem with her body.

People always ranted on about her having a great figure, but Patricia could not see it. According to her, her body was revolting. She could not bear to look at herself in the mirror, because all she saw was the reflection of a fat, unattractive woman staring right back at her. She could never understand why men were attracted to her, because according to her, she was "unattractive, flabby and cursed with the dreaded cellulite". She constantly thought, "If only I could lose some more weight, I would look better." In her efforts to lose weight, Patricia tried every diet or fad on the market to try to burn, dissolve or suck up her fat. She even tried numerous pills she saw advertised on TV, all in the effort to lose weight. Religiously, she hit the scales at least five times a day.

Patricia's efforts did pay off and she went down a few dress sizes. In fact, her weight had been plummeting for the past few years. The story was always the same. Once she reached her target weight, she would say, "I'm too fat," even though her size two clothes were beginning to look too big for her. Patricia was never satisfied. In her mind, all she could see was the fat woman she had once been.

Her friends had lost count of how many times they had tried to reason with her and they had finally given up. So the subject was never raised anymore. Also, to avoid prying eyes, Patricia kept her problem a secret. She went out to eat in the trendiest of places with her girlfriends; but then she would visit the ladies' room to remove the contents of her stomach by vomiting. As soon as she got home, she took a couple of laxatives to remove the remaining contents of her stomach. "At least I won't gain weight," she told herself.

Because she always had her food elimination process to fall back on, Patricia also had a tendency to binge every so often. After gorging herself, she would feel guilty and stop eating for a few days, until she was so weak from lack of nourishment that she was almost passing out. She always dismissed her faintness to her friends with one excuse or another. So it was no surprise that this beautiful attorney, set to be the youngest partner in her firm, collapsed on her way to work one day. It had been twelve days since she had eaten, after yet another binge eating session.

Soon enough, Patricia found herself in a rehab clinic, trying to get herself back together. As for becoming a partner in her law firm, she had no choice but to kiss that dream goodbye for the time being. She heard through the grapevine that her colleague was made partner instead. "That should have been me," she thought as she lay in her clinic bed. It took Patricia many months to put her life back in order and deal with her love-hate relationship with her body and food. Moreover, after many years of dieting, abusing her body and popping dubious pills from TV adverts, she now has to battle a number of health concerns.

"I WANT MY DADDY"

Tracey, a bubbly 16-year-old girl, was full of life. Like any girl of her age, she had big dreams. Her dream was to become a top fashion journalist. Her parents were very supportive. She would have made it into fashion college, since she had a flair for the subject, except for the news that would change her life forever. She was pregnant.

Tracey had never contemplated becoming pregnant at the age of sixteen. When she arrived home from the clinic, she curled up on the floor by her bed and cried, "I want my daddy!" She had come to know that spot on the floor well, as she had cried herself to sleep there for the best part of ten years.

Tracey assumed that, had her father been around, he would have protected her from Uncle Ben, her father's brother, who had been babysitting her since she was six, when her mother had to go to meetings. Uncle Ben had been touching her in ways a little girl ought not to have been touched. It started off as childish playfulness, but even at the age of six, she knew things were not right when he started exposing himself to her. Shortly after that, he started sexually abusing her. He made her promise never to tell anyone about their little secret.

Her only escape had been to stay over at friends' houses. Of course, her girlfriends got a tad fed up with her endless sleepovers, so she took to hanging out at the mall. It was there that she met Tony, a handsome twenty-one-year-old college student. But that only lasted a few weeks. Then, even though she was not of age, she dated David (27), Robert (33), Jay (24) and several others all within a few months.

It would not have been so bad if her pregnancy had been her only worry. Of course, she did not know who the father was — though Uncle Ben's recent antics made him a likely suspect. But there was worse news to come.

She was HIV positive. Tracey stared at the clinic nurse in disbelief. "But I'm only sixteen. How could this be happening to me?" She had never felt so alone. In despair, she felt the tears streaming down her face.

As usual, her mom was out at her Monday night meeting. As for her dad, who knew when he was coming back home? She understood that he had to travel, but she really needed her father to wrap his big arms around her right now. Had he been here, she felt she would never have been driven into the arms of the many men who took advantage of her. Now her dreams were all dashed away and her future looked bleak…all because her daddy had never been around.

WHEN HOPE LOST HER FAITH

Hope picked herself up off the bathroom floor where she had spent the night. Taking a glance into the mirrored medicine cabinet, she saw a painful reminder of the night before. It was supposed to have been a romantic evening, one she had been planning for weeks. She had set the scene carefully: candles everywhere, the fireplace roaring, satin sheets on the bed with rose petals scattered romantically all over them. All that had been missing was her man. She had reminded Kelvin a zillion times to be home on time that night because she had a surprise in store for him. "Maybe this evening will rekindle the fires of our marriage," she had thought as she'd hurried through the house making her final preparations.

Hope had been married for less than a year, yet things seemed to be getting worse by the day. It wouldn't have been so bad, if only Kelvin had come home in the evenings. She wouldn't have minded if he was working late to save up a deposit for their dream home, but that wasn't the case at all! He was out partying like a seasoned bachelor. Strip joints, clubs, bars — you name it, he did it. "But all of that's behind us now", Hope dreamed. "We'll reconnect tonight." She hoped so, for Kelvin had hardly touched her in months!

As Hope stared at her battered and bruised face in the bathroom mirror, it all came back to her. Not only had the evening lacked even a hint of romance, but she had ended up locking herself in the bathroom. Kelvin had come home just after midnight and had not even apologized. The food had long been ruined. To make matters worse, he stank from a concoction of alcohol and perfume. She knew he'd been with another woman.

She'd known Kelvin was a womaniser since the day she'd met him. He had even had the nerve to hit on her maid of honour on their wedding day. But Hope had turned a blind eye to his behaviour, convinced that she could change him. After all, he had picked her to be his bride. She thought that meant something.

Now she was standing in front of the mirror with cuts and bruises on her face. Her face was completely disfigured because of the swelling. She knew she probably had some broken ribs too, judging by the pain on her side. When she had confronted Kelvin, he had beaten her. It wasn't the first time this had happened. Kelvin had hit her a few times before, but it was only because she had made him angry – or so she believed.

Now she would have to face her family, friends and co-workers who would be ready to say, "We told you so". She had already fallen out with her best friend of twenty-five years over Kelvin. Her siblings had boycotted the wedding because they could see she was headed for a great fall. Of course, they had all tried to tell her, but she'd had enough of being single, waiting and waiting with not as much as a date in years. So how could she live this down? "I made a mistake and I don't know what to do," she thought, as tears flowed down her face.

☙

Let me begin by saying that all these characters are fictitious, so you can stop worrying about them. But obviously they are very real representations of what goes on in the lives of many women today – Christians and non-Christians alike. In the scenarios I have narrated, all of these women were Christians.

MORE ON ROBERTA

Roberta, the woman with the broken marriage and the drinking problem, had been a Christian for twenty-five years. She was in a relationship with Richard when she first started going to church. She felt her incredibly good-looking boyfriend was leading her into temptation, but she slept with him anyway. Later on, she found it difficult to live with the guilt and shame she felt about sleeping with her boyfriend, while loving God with all her heart. Fed up with shame, guilt and condemnation, she finally told Richard she could no longer sleep with him. At first, he was OK with it, but the relationship fizzled out shortly afterward. Since then she'd had a string of relationships, but none of them had lasted.

In the meantime, Roberta had settled into her home church, where she was well-known and highly respected. For a number of years, Roberta had been in charge of teaching Bible class and had done a great job of it. All the while, she wondered when she would get married. Like many women she knew, she had never expected she would one day be thirty and unmarried — let alone forty. Roberta's heart was set on waiting for God to bring along her Mr. Right, but the years kept rolling by.

So when Michael came her way, it was as if God had finally answered her cries. Michael had become a Christian and started attending her church. When he attended her Bible classes, they took a fancy to one another. The rest was history. She was soon swept off her feet and head-over-heels in love with him. Although she kept praying and attending church, love overcame her better judgment. Michael popped the question after a few months of dating and they got married on her forty-second birthday that year.

When he left her, it was for his new "soul mate", who also attended the same church and was a close friend of Roberta's.

When Roberta experienced rejection, she went into a frenzy because of her fear of being alone. Her life as an only child had been bad enough, but when her father had walked out on her mother when she was ten years old, she had felt as though he had abandoned her as well. Since her mother became the main breadwinner, Roberta often found herself alone in the house, fending for herself. Her issues with rejection and her deep sense of loneliness had almost driven Roberta over the edge a few times. However, she had always found comfort with alcohol. This was how she had come to have a dependency problem in the first place. It had taken many years, but she had eventually sobered up.

Roberta had had some happy times, but these seemed to only occur whenever she had a man in her life – and none of them seemed to stick around. This intensified her issues of feeling rejected and lonely. Roberta didn't realize that the men who became close to her could immediately sense her neediness over having a man in her life. It came across to them as desperation. This turned off some men, while others relished the opportunity to manipulate her.

Richard had been different. He had looked past all of that to see a beautiful woman. The only problem was that three years down the line, the beautiful woman he had originally met had shrunk into the background, and he found himself with a needy woman. He could never understand why she always wanted them to be together — all the time! She tended to smother him and was very possessive. It unnerved him, and he couldn't take it anymore. He was secretly glad when Roberta said she did not want to sleep with him. It was his way out.

Each time a man left her, Roberta internalised it as rejection. Her tendency was to turn to the bottle. Of course, all this did was mask her issues and provide her with something to buffer her pain. In the meantime, her issues remained. They spewed into her marriage and contributed to its failure.

MORE ON PATRICIA

As for Patricia, she was one of the choir leaders in her home church. She had started out singing as a child in the children's choir, but her amazing ability to capture people's hearts through her angelic voice led to her singing in the adult choir at a young age.

Patricia came from a loving Christian home. She was overweight as a child and spent most of her teen years being teased or jeered at. Patricia was larger than kids who were years older than her. This meant she had no real friends growing up. Worse still, she never had a boyfriend till she was in college. And even then she believed the guy either felt sorry for her or he was just plain weird! From then on, she vowed never to be the butt of people's jokes as long as she lived.

She was haunted by these experiences to such a degree that she eventually blocked out the gentle whispers of the Holy Spirit regarding her eating regimen. For Patricia, it was only too easy to declare long periods of fasting — after all, food meant nothing to her and she could go for days on end without it, all in the name of the Lord. No one in her church or her firm could have guessed what she was putting her body through. As far as they knew, she had it all together!

MORE ON TRACEY

Sixteen-year-old Tracey had spent most of her life in church. Her father had been a travelling preacher for as long as she could remember, while her mother had several key roles in their church. These were the meetings she was always attending. In all of Tracey's years, she had never spent more than five days straight with her father before he went on yet another one of his conferences or speaking engagements. He had been on the road for over ten years running and had rarely gotten to spend time with his children. Though Tracey was "daddy's little girl", she had gotten accustomed to him not being around much and treasured the little time they had together.

In the ten years her father had been away, Tracey accompanied her family to church every Sunday and Wednesday. Although she continued to attend church, there was so much going on in the mind of this sixteen-year-old that she had stopped listening to the preacher many years ago. "Surely, if God loved me, He would not take my daddy away all the time", she thought. Moreover, she told herself that Uncle Ben would not have had the chance to do what he had been doing for years if her daddy had been around.

She felt like her father was out there saving the world, but not around when she needed a saviour from all she had been through. Who else was she supposed to turn to? It would have been different if he were dead or her parents were separated; then she could possibly understand. But it seemed like all he ever did was to come home to change his suitcase and — before she could blink — he was out the door again. If she could have had just one wish, it would have been to have a whole day with her dad. Was that too much to ask?

It's easy to imagine the dilemma parents face as they strive to juggle raising children with fulfilling their own aspirations. However, parents still have a godly responsibility to their children. This subject matter needs to be carefully thought through and the priorities considered wisely, or else the consequences are that children such as Tracey end up suffering for the remainder of their lives.

MORE ON HOPE

The story of Hope is a familiar one. I believe far too many women around the world can relate to her plight as a battered wife.

Hope was an active member in her church. Owing to her medical background, she had helped in initiating many church and community health-related programs. However, her loneliness was always eating away inside her. She had wondered why God was taking so long to bring her the man of her dreams. Had she not fasted and prayed enough? She knew she had a great job with great prospects. However, the one thing missing in her life was a man to enjoy life with.

After all these years of doing the right thing and keeping herself pure, she thought God would have sorted her out by now. Year in, year out, she watched all of her siblings get married and start families. The story was the same in church, too. All the younger ones were bypassing her. It did not help that she seemed to be spending most of her weekends at engagement parties, bridal showers and baby showers. "Lord, what about me?" was her constant cry.

As she approached her fortieth birthday, Hope began to worry. She had never been one to think about biological clocks, but hers seemed to be ringing all the time. These thoughts plagued her mind night and day. Eventually, they wore her down. It came to a point where she became despondent and cynical about God's ability to deal with her situation. With her trust in God diminishing, church simply became a religious duty performed to get people off her case.

It did not help that every time a church member came her way, they would say, "This is your year, Sister Hope!" She would smile and dutifully retort, "Amen!" even though what she really meant was, "Whatever!" Deep inside, Hope no longer believed. When she had the energy, she cried out to God saying, "I want to be a wife. I want a man of my own. Is that too much to ask for, Lord?" Hope never thought she would get so low. She had even spent previous years encouraging other women in similar situations. And now, here she was, discouraged, with her well of faith running dry.

In her desperation, she decided to help God out. She called it putting faith to her actions. However, her emotions were in the driving seat, dictating her decisions. It seemed that there was no ready supply of brothers in church, so she thought she would look elsewhere. Kelvin was an attractive businessman she had met some time back who had been pestering her for a date. He seemed genuine enough and seemed to like her. So she grabbed the business card that had been sitting on her bookshelf for ages and called him up. She agreed to go out with the dishy entrepreneur. Before she knew what had happened, they were an item. She had long brushed aside the still voice within her warning her of the trap ahead. When he proposed soon afterwards, it was no surprise that she said, "Yes".

> *Each row, pew and seat is occupied with women and men trying to make sense of what is going on in their worlds.*

When she introduced Kelvin, her pastor pulled her aside and warned her against marrying him. Her mother also sensed a problem and begged her not to marry him. She encouraged Hope in the fact that God was still able to make a way, for she had been praying for Hope's godly husband from the day she was born. Unperturbed by all the warnings, which were rife, Hope married Kelvin. Her mother cried throughout the wedding ceremony. Less than a year later, Hope had been beaten black and blue by her unsaved husband.

Sister, perhaps you're not aware of it, but these scenarios happen every day – even in our churches. Just like the world at large, the church is full of real people with real problems. Each row, pew and seat is occupied with women and men trying to make sense of what is going on in their worlds. They cope as well as they can, but often their coping behaviours fail them. And all of a sudden, they have yet more problems to worry about. The pain is real, Sister — as real as you and me.

ENLIGHTENING MOMENT

Looking For Restoration In The Wrong Places

If you take a moment to pause and reflect, can you relate to any of the scenarios above? It could be that you have survived an ordeal or two in the past. Or maybe you're dealing with a situation right now. Wherever you are today, I encourage you to seek help in the right places. As you can see, our emotional baggage affects our behaviours, attitudes, beliefs and decisions. Ultimately, it can ruin our lives. Notice that all these women appeared to be all right on the outside, but had so many problems going on inside them. You can now begin to see how emotional baggage can railroad you off your path to a successful, purposeful and fulfilled life – especially if you continue to sprint through life without checking in with yourself. Please also bear in mind that your emotional restoration depends on what or who you turn to in order to steady the boat or calm the storms in your life. Now is a good time to reflect on what's going on in your life.

PART 4

The Origins Of The Female Hybrid

Chapter Eight

In Search Of Eden

O n my personal journey away from being a female hybrid, God taught me some valuable lessons. As I was starting to decelerate from my fast-paced life, I started to take note of what He was sharing with me. When I finally sat still enough to ponder these lessons, I realised that everything was pointing toward one simple thing — the beginning. By the word *beginning*, I am referring to the very beginning — God's creation of the world.

I soon figured out that God was trying to remind me of the original plans He had for humankind when He created us. I felt prodded to revisit the Book of Genesis, the Book that tells us how the world was created.

It became obvious to me that if I could revisit the beginning, it would give me a taste of the life God had in mind for us. Then I could understand how to help women start to retrace our steps with a view to becoming the original women God had in mind, instead of *female hybrids*.

There is a Yoruba (Nigerian) proverb which says, "If you can't seem to make progress forward, consider retracing your steps and go back to where you came from."

Remembering that gave me a sudden moment of insight. I knew it made sense to stop sprinting, stand still and look over my shoulder to retrace my journey. Without doing that, many of us discover we are way off track when it is too late.

I soon realised that my initial task was to do a form of spiritual benchmarking. The only way to do that was to step back in time and revisit the Garden of Eden. Let's go there together now. Back in time … in search of Eden.

ଔ

Imagine you're taking a stroll through the most amazing garden in this world. The sun's warm rays pierce through the branches of magnificent trees and warm your face. Walking barefoot, you cannot but notice the soft, luscious blades of grass. You are surrounded by the most breathtaking display of flowers of every colour, shape and size. Their fragrant aroma fills the air around you. There are trees of every kind, too; many with succulent fruit, ready for eating. The garden comes alive with the harmonious singing and chirping of an array of beautifully coloured birds. Two fluffy white baby rabbits cross your path, one chasing the other in a carefree manner; they play by the spring. To your right, beside the huge oak tree, a newborn lamb leans against its mother. Other animals can be seen grazing, playing or simply hanging out with each other in perfect harmony. The garden exudes a serene atmosphere.

Into the scene come Adam and Eve, living together in bliss. You can tell they are in love by the way they gaze into each other's eyes. They walk hand in hand through the enchanted Eden, their hearts as one. No raised voices or arguments can be heard, just loving conversations between two people who appreciate the gift God has given them in each other. Because of their love and appreciation, neither is out to dominate or ill-treat the other. In fact there are no egos, tempers, mood swings or emotional issues anywhere in sight. Both are committed to supporting each other in fulfilling God's pre-ordained job specification of being fruitful, multiplying and tending the garden (Genesis 1:27-28 and 2:15).

This sounds great, doesn't it? This is my kind of life.

I guess by now you are probably thinking, "What planet is she on? Hello! This is the twenty-first century, girlfriend!" I hear you! I appreciate that things have changed somewhat since then. In fact, I'll go one step further to say things have actually changed drastically. It's true we no longer live in a garden, and most of us don't spend our time hanging out with animals. We live in a technological era with gadgets to do just about everything for us. Scientifically, we have become more advanced than any other age in the history of man. However, with all these great achievements, the world has never been so spiritually depraved. And as for the state of our souls — our emotional well-being — they are in a constant state of alert!

While the environment we live in has changed drastically, I do not believe that it was God's intention for our internal state to change from what He originally planned. And just because we have deviated from God's original plan does not mean that His plans have changed for us. Let's look into this more closely.

GOD'S ORIGINAL SPECIFICATION FOR HUMANKIND

First, we have to accept the fact that what we know of Adam, Eve and Eden is real according to the Bible. This was how Adam and Eve actually lived before sin came onto the scene. Maybe I stretched the story a little about the romantic side of things, but I assure you, I was probably not too far off. Secondly, when God created Adam and Eve, all aspects of their tripartite beings were in a healthy state and working in harmony with each other, not in isolation. Therefore, I reiterate the fact that God had a healthy and balanced version of you in mind when He created you. Our task is to retrace our steps back to that place of wholeness in every sense of the word. Let's take a closer look.

THE SPIRITUAL BEING

One of the things that I noticed immediately is the fact that both Adam and Eve had a relationship with God. They connected with Him on a regular basis as God took strolls in the garden to visit His created beings. It was not the case that they were so preoccupied with the tasks He gave them to do that they abandoned their spiritual connectivity with Him. Now I know things are different now; many of us will go through our lives without having a physical encounter with God like Adam and Eve did. However, He has instituted a direct form of relationship and communication through the promised Holy Spirit. Before Jesus left the earth, He promised to send the Holy Spirit Who would remain here on earth with us. Through the Holy Spirit, we can connect with God Who is a Spirit. Therefore we could also have this same relationship the first people had with God.

However, it helps to bear in mind that in the same way sin affected the relationship between God and man after the fall, our sins today can equally drive a wedge between our Creator and us. But thankfully, we have a forgiving God we can call upon for forgiveness to heal and restore our right standing with Him through Jesus Christ. Therefore, our obligation is to recognise our need to be connected with God and connect with Him regularly. This links in with my first two principles: *Get God Involved Right From The Start!* and *Learn To Connect With Others.*

THE EMOTIONAL BEING

Prior to their fall, we see no aspect of Adam and Eve's lives being out of balance. All their personal needs were met, which tells us that their actions were not motivated by a lack of some sort in their lives.

I envision Adam as a self-assured man who had no emotional issues, even after Eve came on the scene. Even though he'd had all of God's attention to himself before her arrival, he wasn't concerned about her stealing the show. I see him as a provider and a hard worker, although not excessively so, determined to honour and care for the companion God had so graciously given him. I'm sure he would have remembered all too well his single days when he had no one to add zest to his life. All he had for companions were the animals. And when suddenly the "bone of his bones and flesh of his flesh" arrived, he cherished her as a gift from God. No thoughts of domination, cruelty, selfishness or coldness crossed his mind, as he knew Eve was fashioned by the very hands of God and was made in His image, too.

As for Eve, I am convinced that she had no emotional problems about her weight, size, shape or complexion. After all, she and Adam were walking around naked! Neither had any emotional imbalances they had to compensate for. I believe we can safely assume that Adam and Eve were not carrying any of the emotional baggage many seem to be carrying around with them today such as low self-esteem, unresolved problems, unmet needs, compulsive behaviours and so on.

Over time I have built up a personal image of Eve. I imagine a confident woman with an understanding of her own identity. She knew she was handcrafted by God Himself and she walked in that authority. There was nothing pretentious or fake about her. She did not have the *female hybrid* tendencies or have the need to wear a mask. She was not a needy, emotional, attitude-oriented, mouthy or domineering woman. I don't know about you, but I have not read anywhere that Eve had a tendency to go off in a sulk and do her own thing. Can you imagine Eve declaring to Adam, "I'm an independent woman and I don't need a man!'"? We are not informed of her ever retreating to another part of the garden, not wanting to see Adam because she couldn't stand him or even giving him the silent treatment. Nor do we find her running off to her girlfriends (or should I say animal friends?), yapping away about how Adam has just gotten on her last nerve.

I believe that Adam and Eve were at peace within themselves and with each other. Why? Because this was how God Almighty created them and ordained things to be.

This is the way God created all of us to live, regardless of our present realities. He also ordained us to continue to live in this fashion till the end of time. In considering this idea, it has become clearer to me that the state we often find ourselves in today is not how God wants us to remain. After all, from the standards He set for us when He created the first people, tells us that this is not His best for us, which reinforced principle four: *Don't Settle Where You Are.*

THE PHYSICAL BEING

Even though the Bible does not go into depth about what Adam and Eve looked like, you can be sure they were the quintessence of man and woman, just the way God had in mind. If God can state that what He created was excellent in every way (Genesis 1:31), then I am fully persuaded that all He created was, indeed, outstanding and in good working order. Personally, I believe this was the standard He set for us to live by.

Focusing on their physical bodies, we see no evidence of them abusing their bodies through poor eating habits or stress by being always on the go. This afforded them the time and energy to build their relationships with each other and with God. I assume they adopted God's idea of the Sabbath rest just the same way God did. By doing this, they did not stand a chance of stress or physical burn-out, which is a prevalent problem today, both in the church and the secular world.

One other aspect of the physical side is the fact that Adam and Eve were both focused on their assignments. Another word for our assignment is our *purpose.*

By the time we are born, we each have a purpose here on earth. The trick is to connect with the One who sent us here in the first place. Personally, I find it difficult to hear God's voice when I am sprinting through life or am preoccupied physically or emotionally. Chances are that after sprinting, I am tired and not in my peak condition. This means I may be prone to making the wrong choices. Or I may not hear His voice because of clutter that has accumulated in my mind through my constantly being and doing.

That's why I value taking regular retreats that can last from a few hours to as long as I feel I need. Doing this allows me to check in with myself to find out what I have been up to — to evaluate, refocus, strategize and rest. These days, it's just so easy to get sucked up in the rat race of life. A lot of people do it. But I do believe things don't have to be that way. That's why I mentioned earlier that the abundant life that Adam and Eve were living was my own heart's desire. I believe this can be achieved and I am determined to continue to change the rules of my life to permit me to do this.

In regard to our purpose in life, another trap many people seem to fall into today is that they either don't know what their purpose is and end up doing things that lie outside of their purpose, or they know what their purpose is and may even start doing it, but ultimately latch on to other tasks that shift their focus and steer them off track. And of course, there are those who fit into the all-or-nothing category of people who either go for their purpose wholeheartedly or those who don't do anything at all. That's why I find principles three and five so relevant: *Take Time To Develop Yourself* and *Focus On Your Purpose – Not Your Agenda!*

β

I am hoping that you are beginning to see some trends in terms of God's intentions for our lives. Now I accept that things are a tad different. For example, it is not clear as to whether Adam and Eve even had childhoods. We are told that God formed man from the dust of the ground (Genesis 2:7) and Eve from Adam's rib (Genesis 2: 21-23). For a number of adults with unresolved problems today, a percentage of these originate from their childhood. There are those who have had a great childhood, but have picked up their unresolved problems from their day-to-day life experiences since then. The end result is that both groups of people face opportunities for their beings to be out of balance. However, this is where the five principles I mentioned earlier come into play.

So regardless of your background, you do not have to remain the way you are. By focusing on God's original plan for your life, you can retrace your steps and start living the life He set out for you.

JOURNALING MOMENT

What Part Of You Is Out Of Sync?

Now that you have had an opportunity to revisit Eden, take some time to write you're your thoughts. Under the headings of "spirit", "soul" and "body", make a list of specific examples highlighting where you feel you have become out of balance.

_____

_____

_____

_____

_____

_____

Chapter Nine

The Birth Of The Female Hybrid

*B*ased on what we have covered so far, I believe Adam and Eve's tripartite beings were in good working order and were working in unison. However, things changed with the introduction of an external factor – an internalised message. For Eve, the message she internalised turned out to be a deceptive lie from the serpent (Genesis 3:1-7). We read on to see that Eve passed on the deceptive lie (i.e., the forbidden fruit) to her husband Adam. This was the beginning of the fall of mankind (Genesis 3) and the birth of the troubled soul.

Today, other internalised messages in the form of people's opinions, popular beliefs, deceptive lies, fads, false doctrines and traditions of men continue to wreak havoc in the lives of many people, bringing them out of balance. These messages are passed on to others, propagating these issues in the lives of others. When you couple the internalised messages with other external factors such as adverse personal experiences both past and present, we see mankind becoming more troubled. And so we see large numbers of female hybrids tottering about with their emotional baggage of differing shapes and sizes.

Immediately after the eyes of Adam and Eve were opened, they became ashamed. The first thing they did was not to look for God, but to try to find some way of getting rid of the feelings of nakedness, shame and guilt. So what did they do? They stitched together fig leaves to cover their shame (Genesis 3:7). This provided immediate relief from how they felt, but it did not take their problem away. It only gave them a temporary relief along with the illusion that the matter had now been resolved. If only the fig leaves we use in our lives had this ability! However, we know that this is not the case. Our fig leaves have a short life span. Once they wear out, we are confronted with the very thing we were trying to escape, mask over or numb ourselves to. The cycle starts yet again as we use more and more of our "fig leaf", our doping agent, to escape it all. Shortly, even bigger cracks appear, prompting us to start increasing the use of our temporary gap fillers or seek the use of new ones. Sadly, many lose relationships, families, fortunes and even their lives this way.

The appearance of sin in the Garden of Eden opened many doors to the contents of our emotional baggage. Because of what happened in Eden, we have seen sin's effects travel down generations, from biblical times through our present day. In our efforts to restore ourselves to our original state, the many precarious approaches adopted have only left even bigger cracks. The reason is that these methods have left God out of the equation. I know because I have tried this and failed woefully. Others have done the same, only to realise that our DIY, self-help approaches open a whole new can of worms.

Remember the saying, "a little yeast leavens the bread" (Galatians 5:9)? Well, let's just say that what started out as one issue has been known to blow up into many life-shattering, generation-destroying issues. Please bear in mind that trying to perform DIY surgery on your soul can be dangerous. It makes better sense to hand it over to a specialist who has a track record of healing troubled souls. After all, is the Bible not full of these kinds of people?

Sister, it is high time we begin to recognize the antics of the serpent who is still operating today by whispering into the ears of many and snaring them with the forbidden fruit. We can no longer afford this in our lives because it detracts from the women God created us to be. We need to turn our backs on the devil, identify what's not right in our lives, and find our true place of solace in God. Only He can restore us back to the way He designed us to be.

JOURNALING AND ENLIGHTENING MOMENT

Which Forbidden Fruit Have You Bitten Into Lately?

We looked at the story of Eve and saw how the serpent deceived her into eating the forbidden fruit. My questions to you are as follows:

What's going on in your own garden — what fruit is being used to tempt you?

What messages have you internalised?

What forbidden fruit have you been munching on lately?

_____

_____

_____

_____

_____

_____

_____

_____

_____

_____

_____

_____

_____

_____

_____

_____

_____

_____

_____

_____

_____

_____

_____

_____

_____

_____

_____

Now is a good time to reflect on your own life. So pause and take stock of what may have been used to deceive you into becoming a female hybrid.

Chapter Ten

Modern Dilemmas Of A Female Hybrid

*W*omen have been fondly called the emotional ones of the human species. There is some truth in this. Frankly speaking, Sister, we are different from men and God intended it that way. You may have noticed that we operate in different ways. We think, behave and express ourselves differently, too. That is the way things are supposed to be. We were never meant to be the same. So why is it that many of us find it difficult to be real women? Could it be that we have internalized messages that influence how we see ourselves?

One of these messages says that if we want to succeed in a man's world, we need to toughen up and be aggressive. I can understand being assertive, but I do not have to lose my delicate femininity over it. A number of these messages have been covertly delivered to us since childhood.

We all heard as children, "Stop crying! Only babies cry!" Many girls and boys have interpreted this to mean, "If you cry, you will be seen as weak, unable, helpless or inadequate".

I have to admit that I fell for this one. For years, I would not cry in front of people – not even my own biological sisters, let alone anyone else! Moreover, I did not want the devil thinking he had finally worn me down. I seemed to have internalized some external unspoken law that said, "Thou shalt not cry – regardless." For me, it had that connotation of weakness, hopelessness and defeat. I certainly did not want to be perceived like that. In reality, I was far from being a weak, hopeless or defeated person. But you know what it is like when your mind is caught up with some notion after giving your ears to the enemy. What you believe in eventually becomes a part of you. It was later that God used various avenues such as sound teaching and godly relationships to make me realise that crying is a release of emotions that include happiness, sadness, anger and frustration that God Himself instigates. Moreover, Jesus wept! (John 11:35) I rest my case.

So many of us embark on our life journeys trying to show how resilient we are – based on this message alone. If we were to gather all the different messages we have internalized all our lives, you can begin to see the repercussions.

It's no wonder there are female hybrids! We keep internalising messages that are untrue and that contradict God's Word. The more we keep doing this, the less of us remains from our original version. The female clone may have internalized a message that said, "The person you were created to be is not good enough for our standards." The female chameleon may have listened to a message that said, "To join our group and be one of us, you have to be or do XYZ." The female masquerader may have been told, "Expose your real self, feelings or pain and you will lose the respect of others." In the case of the female superhero, I can hear her thinking, "If I give more and more of what I want, others will give the same back to me." As for our female pessimist, she might have heard someone say, "Why bother trying? You will fail anyway." The possibility for internalizing wrong messages is endless.

LIFE SITUATIONS

To complicate matters, let's throw in some more life situations, such as divorce, broken relationships, abuse, sickness and other personal setbacks. These can quickly contribute to the emotional baggage you are already carrying about with you. I don't know about you, but the old me would have endeavoured to brush these crises aside and get on with my sprinting through life as soon as I could.

Now while God tells us many times in the Bible to "be strong and courageous" (Joshua 1:6-7, 9; First Corinthians 16:13), "keep standing" (Ephesians 6:13), and "stand firm" (Second Thessalonians 2:15), He does not deny the fact that we will go through some personal crises that will require Him to rescue us. Was this not the reason why Jesus came to the world — to save the lost and heal the sick? Is there a need for a physician if there is no sickness? Is there a need for a Saviour if there is nothing anyone needs to be saved from? The answer is no.

You might want to browse through the Scriptures to all the passages where He spoke about healing. There are loads of Scriptures concerning the lonely, broken-hearted, despised and rejected, and God providing comfort to them. (See Psalm 34:18, Psalm 68:6, Isaiah 51:3, Isaiah 61:1-3, Isaiah 66:13, Jeremiah 31:10-13, Second Corinthians 1:3-5.) So why do we try to keep up the façade that everything's cool with us when we are falling to pieces on the inside? Don't we need to tap into some of what God has in store for His own?

Not dealing with the contents of your emotional baggage and the messages you have internalized over the years will have an impact on you. And no, Sister, this is not a negative declaration, but a matter of fact! Want proof? The story of Saul and his insecurities comes to mind. Remember, it was because of Saul's tragedies that David was appointed as the next king over Israel. Better still, you can choose to conduct your own little experiment and do nothing about your own situation and reassess it in five, ten and fifteen years. I would not recommend the last option, however, as you only have one shot at life.

Sister, we need to understand that it is not a macho or spiritual thing for women (or men, for that matter) to deny the truth about the realities in our lives. There are no superheroes, especially for those who still occupy an earthly body. I guess that includes all of us.

THE MAKING OF A FEMALE HYBRID

The effect of not pausing to look inwardly or even being real with ourselves means that many of us have a huge number of emotions pent up, suppressed, denied or ignored as we strive to make it in life. Moreover, we don't do a great deal about these emotions.

This is the reason for the disappearance of the real woman and the proliferation of the female hybrid.

Sadly, this rapid proliferation means we find female hybrids in all walks of life. They run businesses, homes and ministries. They are on the pages of glossy magazines and on our televisions. They are also found in our offices and churches. It appears that this emerging pattern knows no boundaries and is indiscriminate.

I will never forget two separate occasions, many years ago, when I was consulting with two corporations. In both situations, I had to work very closely with clients who happened to be high-powered female senior managers with a lot of clout — and unresolved problems.

These female hybrids were a nightmare to work with, to put it mildly. Having meetings with these women was a dreadful experience, because I could typically count on them to shout, bang their fists on tables, dish out inexplicable rudeness to all and sundry, storm off during workshops and generally behave in rude and unprofessional ways. I tell you, these hybrids had some men quivering in their boots. To appease them, people simply gave in to their demands no matter how ridiculous they were.

Personally, I was appalled to see this. Normally, when I see women soar in their careers and take on high positions in an organization, I am leaping for joy internally. I like to see women progress and I feel that it should be celebrated, especially in a world where we face so many obstacles in reaching these positions. However, I get equally disappointed when such individuals give a poor representation of the greatness of the women God created. It grieves me to the core. I really feel strongly about the responsibility those in leadership positions have regardless of whether they lead in the home, office, corporation or church. They were appointed by God and have an obligation both to Him and to the people they lead to lead effectively. This means dealing with their own personal issues to help them become better in their roles. It's not their subordinates', children's or congregation members' fault if they have been abused, abandoned or rejected at some point in their lives. So why take it out on them or make their lives a living nightmare working with you? It is essential that such women deal with these issues rather than have their issues drive them to become female hybrids. As for the rest of the Sisters out there who are not in leadership positions, they must also endeavour to be the best they can be. This means working on themselves and ridding themselves of any emotional baggage that can trip them up.

I have come to the conclusion after working with women for so long that the female hybrid pattern is a real issue we cannot afford to take lightly. Because what's been happening from ages past is that the real woman is being silently hacked – stripped away of the essence of our womanhood. What we see today is a crossbreed between the original person God created and one the external environment has fashioned. Sadly, many are unaware of this transmutation.

From my biology classes, I remember that some mutations are beneficial to organisms. These mutations help the organism survive better in their natural environments. In the case of female hybrids, the mutation is not beneficial. If anything, it adds up to our demise because of the patterns we must adopt to deal with all of the emotional baggage that comes with that mutation.

CONSEQUENCES OF BEING A FEMALE HYBRID

By not taking out the time to work on yourself, as opposed to your business, career, family or church, you stand a chance of failing to accomplish God's purpose for you. Moreover, your life will be marred with negative emotions and behaviours that will spill into other areas of your life.

Ever wondered why your relationships keep failing, you keep picking the wrong guy, you are struggling with your weight, you are trapped in habits of the past you keep promising never to do again, you often feel down when you have much to celebrate, your finances are just out of control, your business or career is not going in the direction you want it to go or your life is not going according to plan?

These emotional symptoms have dogged the lives of many women, including mine. Yet our response is to work harder at steadying our boats or simply finding new ways to keep them afloat. What I suggest is that you press pause for a moment and ask yourself: Are you happy to expend all that energy for the rest of your life doing this?

Have you ever noticed that when you drive your car at high speeds, the engine burns a lot more fuel? When you also overload the car, you make the engine work even harder. With the car being overloaded and speeding, would the engine not have to work even harder to cover the same distance as if it would have done with no excess baggage and no excessive speeds? Ponder that.

JOURNALING MOMENT

Who Have You Become?

Consider responding to the following as truthfully as you can:

What messages have you internalized over the years?
Where did they originate?
What impact has this had on your life?

_____

_____

_____

_____

_____

_____

THE ELASTIC BAND STRETCH/SHRINK THEORY

Have you ever been in a position when you were completely stuck? You have all the best intentions in the world and may know what to do, but you can't seem to move forward. It's not as though you have always been like this; you have made progress in the past. Regardless of the support you have around you, you simply cannot shift yourself into gear. In fact, it feels like you are sitting in a bath of solid cement, unable to move. I can relate to this after experiencing the feelings of being in this stuck mode a few times myself.

As a coach, I have worked with a few clients who have found themselves in this place too. They had similar traits. They were keen to accomplish a great deal and even started out great, but no sooner had they embarked on their project than they seemed to find themselves stuck. On the surface there seemed to be no apparent reason as to why they were not getting the results they desired or managing to simply maintain their objectives.

As I began to probe deeper, I soon began to get a clearer picture as to what was going on beneath the surface. I call this phenomenon the elastic band stretch/shrink theory, which is a cyclical pattern.

Imagine yourself on the inside of a giant elastic band that is attached to a stationary post. You start to run. As you pick up speed, you start to stretch the elastic band. At first, you appear to forge ahead – getting on with life and doing great things. Everything seems rosy. You are on top of the world. Through your sprinting, you continue to stretch the elastic till it reaches its limit. This is your stretch mode.

However, as you sprint, your emotional baggage, internalized messages and female hybrid tendencies kick in and make it a bit more difficult to keep up the pace. In addition to this, your day-to-day life experiences also kick in — personal setbacks, broken relationships or anything else that may trigger a reaction from you. And so your pace starts slows down.

Logic tells us that, once you stretch the band to its limit and the force that stretches it (your sprinting) is not maintained, it will eventually return back to its original state. The time this takes will depend on the pace at which you decelerate. As you continue to decelerate, sooner or later, you will find yourself back to square one as the elastic strives to return itself back to its original state. The deceleration process — which will eventually grind you to a halt — is what I term your shrink mode.

It is most likely that during your deceleration phase is where you find you are not able to do or keep up with the great things you were previously achieving. You can't seem to move forward and, if you do, it is not at your usual pace, maximizing your potential. By the time you come to a halt, you find yourself stuck because of the overwhelming nature of the junk you carry around with you. Life becomes a struggle. It is most likely that some negative emotions and emotional symptoms will come out to play.

The elastic band represents all our limiting factors, such as emotional baggage, internalized messages, female hybrid tendencies and day-to-day life experiences that come out to play and interrupt our life journey. Our automatic response is to put more effort into keeping the elastic band stretched continuously. This takes a great deal of effort as you are struggling against many opposing forces (i.e., your limiting factors). Therefore, there is a high chance we start to rely heavily on our coping behaviours and emotional buffers. Eventually, the "elastic bands" of our lives affect our personal effectiveness and productivity and it becomes a contributory factor to our being stuck.

In my search for an answer, I discovered that one of the primary propagators of this cycle is the condition of the person.

When we are in our hybrid state, we are laden with emotional cracks, because the emotional baggage is too heavy for us. Through inadequate time and effort spent repairing the cracks, the cracks get bigger and bigger. Then we go through life like walking wounded, trying to accomplish all these great things, and we wonder why we get stuck.

If you have your eyes on the top or simply want to live a life filled with meaning and fulfilment, your initial efforts must be spent in repairing your cracks and eliminating your emotional baggage along with your other limiting factors before you endeavour to reach for the top. Otherwise, all your efforts would be wasted. This is akin to trying to fill a sieve with water. You will forever keep pouring water in it but never ever filling it. And so, if you care to take a step back, you may find that you have been sprinting with cracks in your stretch mode which have ended up marring your efforts and even contributing to your becoming stuck in your shrink mode. Sister, the truth of the matter is that we need to work on building a healthy foundation before we even consider building a skyscraper on top. After all, we all know what happens to a building with a weak foundation. It tumbles down.

And so when working with clients who may be stuck, we often spend time working on their foundations. Many are sceptical, think it is a bit wishy-washy, counter-productive and feel it is taking the focus off their goals. However, in working together, they experience a lot of light-bulb moments as they come face to face with the reality of their true state and the impact it has or will have on their aspirations. Little do they know how their cracks have impacted their behaviours, attitudes and beliefs.

Over the years I have lost track of how many of my clients have come to me with great dreams and aspirations who, through a process of discovery, took the time to invest in their foundations. Once they were mended, they saw results that were over and above what they had initially set out to accomplish. Previously, I mentioned the case of a particular client who was a highly qualified professional woman whose self-defeating attitudes, beliefs and behaviours meant she was settling for menial or jobs way beneath her. Her goal in working with a coach was to land her dream job. However, it became evident that some foundational work was necessary not only to achieve this goal, but also maintain it. Over a period of time, she began moving out of her stuck mode. In little or no time, she landed her first managerial role. Later on, she landed a lucrative highflying role in a huge organization. As far as I know, she is still soaring!

> ✠
>
> *The trap that many people fall into is going through the stretch / shrink cycle too frequently without pausing to prayerfully reflect.*
>
> ✠

In our shrink mode, if we lack the necessary support mechanisms, we may look for ways to overcome the very things that are catapulting us back to square one. A number of us opt for temporary fillers such as food, thinking they will help us feel better about ourselves. By doing this, we stockpile short-lived remedies rather than putting our efforts into getting our real needs met.

The immediate relief we experience gives us the impression that we are ready for the world again. So we declare that our shrink mode is over and we're back to sprinting again — till we reach our limits and continue the cycle. The time spent between modes can vary from minutes, hours and days to weeks, months and years.

The trap that many people fall into is going through the stretch/shrink cycle too frequently without pausing to prayerfully reflect. We don't give ourselves the allowance to pause on our life's journeys. It's only when we come crashing right back to where we started that we may start to ponder what's going on. Therefore, our aims ought to be eliminating the elastic bands of our lives that keep us trapped in the stretch/shrink cycle.

Another important point to bear in mind is that the chances are while in your stretch mode, the real you is most likely missing in action. This is beside the fact that you seem to be accomplishing a lot.

For example, the female masquerader would probably paint the picture of one who is succeeding in her stretch mode as she has perfected the art of masquerading, hiding the contorts of pain on her face. Hidden by her mask, her real issues are concealed. With her emotional baggage neatly packed away in her designer "eb" luggage, she is ready for the journey. The female superhero will be seen to be doing all her good deeds in her stretch mode, too. The problem occurs when these two female hybrids run out of steam and come crashing to their shrink mode. It's not a pretty sight. That's when the cracks begin to show to all and sundry. Do you wonder how I came to know this so well? Let's just say there was a time in my life I was living in the stretch/shrink cycle myself.

You will do well to bear in mind the fact that it is tough living life oscillating between stretching and shrinking. Many people have discovered that their emotional baggage becomes a stumbling block to living the abundant life promised to us all. I frequently ponder how it is at all possible to pursue our huge aspirations or even our purposes in life with such handicaps.

I remember confronting God with this same question. After all, from my perspective, I could not imagine me or anyone else embarking on the great tasks ahead of us with so much emotional baggage strapped to our backs. Then God reminded me of some of the greatest people He used in the Bible. None of them, with the exception of Jesus, was perfect. In fact, He reminded me that He did not use perfect people, but people who strived for perfection despite their humanity and aimed to be a good reflection of Him. I understood this to mean the following:

- We are to be humble and wise enough to identify with our strengths and limitations (i.e. the good, the bad and the ugly part of our lives).
- We should develop the habit of continuously reviewing and modifying our behaviours, attitudes and beliefs so we can be the image of God.

Through experience, I believe these things can be accomplished by consistently developing our relationships with God via prayer, reading of the Word of God and fellowship with His people. Without this, we may find ourselves caught in the stretch/shrink cycle.

JOURNALING MOMENT

Notice Any Patterns Or Trends?

Following the theme of the last section, take your time in responding to the following questions:

Do you find yourself fluctuating from being emotionally high one day to low another? If so, does this happen regularly or infrequently?

What impact has this had on your life?
What situations trigger these fluctuations? Notice any trends?
How have you endeavoured to handle them?

Take a moment to reflect on the answers you have come up with. Think through the following:

Were any of your answers a surprise to you?

What do you believe is the root cause behind your findings? Is it due to emotional baggage accumulated from your childhood or baggage you picked up through your life experiences?

PRAYING MOMENT

Now I would like you to bring your findings before the Lord in prayer. Ask Him to help you overcome the emotional baggage and patterns of behaviour you have accumulated over time. Remember, only He has a permanent solution.

PART 5

The Propagation Of The Female Hybrid Problem

Chapter Eleven

The Never-Ending Cycles

I don't know about you, but it took many years for me to realize how my emotional baggage had affected me. It was as if it had become a part of my life. I had accepted it as the norm. Of course, I did not really spend too much time trying to get rid of it. I was far too busy for that. I did what many female hybrids do: I perfected the art of masquerade. This resulted in my fluctuation between stretch/shrink modes.

In case you were wondering, I did try to get rid of this baggage. However, no matter what I tried, it simply did not work! This came as no surprise, actually. Remember how I mentioned earlier that for complete emotional recovery, certain mental and spiritual shifts had to take place based on biblical principles? Well, let's just say I had to learn them the hard way! I'll show you what I mean.

Principle One: Get God Involved Right From The Start

Believing in God's supernatural power to heal was never a problem for me. The stories in the Bible were the only proof I needed. However, translating that into a reality in my life was a different story. It was probably due to my female superhero tendencies. I was so used to the idea of saving others that I had begun to internalize the opinion that I could also handle anything that happened to me. It was like an unconscious belief that I was omnipotent – just like a real superhero!

Of course, it was not true – otherwise, I'd have been on equal footing with God and would have had no need for Him. So my superhero tendencies meant I tried to figure things out myself. It was like I was always saying to God, "Don't worry Father, I got this one!"

I had always been independent since childhood. When a problem arose, I did not go to my mummy, daddy, family, friends, boss or pastor. Oh no, that was too easy! I simply tried to fix the problem myself. I was a DIY girl to the core.

As a person, I thrive on challenges. I love insurmountable challenges and new opportunities – the ones most people tend to run from. I love going into unknown territories. When I conquer and succeed in my goals, it gives me a sense of personal satisfaction. So any time I faced a glitch in my personal or professional life, I somehow managed to resolve it single-handedly — most of the time. This could include fixing or installing things around the house.

Only when I got into trouble and could not see my way out would I consider screaming for help and calling in the cavalry (a handyman, a family member or friend) to save this damsel in distress. Trust me, by the time I asked for help, I would have exhausted every ounce of strength and know-how I could muster. I would have struggled and even suffered in silence till it got unbearable. This was how I lived my life in my B.I.R.G.T.K.G. (before I really got to know God) days. So it was no wonder this I-can-fix-it-myself mindset spilled over into my A.D.G. (after discovering God) days.

However, when an emotional issue surfaced, all my efforts appeared to be futile. And so I simply added it to my to-do list and that was that. The only problem was that over the years, my list grew longer and longer as I could do nothing about these kinds of problems. My next tactic was to avoid them and carry on with business as usual. As you may have guessed, business as usual meant sprinting through life. This meant I was running with extra baggage. I even tried to self-coach myself. I would talk frankly to myself saying, "Get over it, woman!" However, nothing worked. Needless to say, the effects of my self-directed motivational speeches only lasted a short while. Sooner or later, the problems would resurface on the to-do list that my mind was collating.

As a result, I was eating rapidly into my spiritual, physical and emotional reserves to evade emotional issues. I never really took the bull by its horns when it came to these matters, as I would have done on other non-related matters. I was simply stuck! I later discovered that regardless of how independent, intelligent or educated I was, I could not eradicate my issues myself. Bottom line, I needed help. And it could not be just any help, but the help of God, the real Superhero!

By doing all these things, I had simply missed the plot! I had not fully grasped the fact that God was my true Healer. Rather than trying to get things done in my own strength, this was a matter in which I was supposed to get God involved right from the start.

ENLIGHTENING MOMENT

Take some time to meditate on the following Scriptures and let them work inside you.

> *I am overcome with joy because of your unfailing love, for you have seen my troubles, and you care about the anguish of my soul.*
>
> Psalm 31:7

The Lord is close to the brokenhearted; he rescues those who are crushed in spirit.

Psalm 34:18

The Lord nurses them when they are sick and eases their pain and discomfort.

Psalm 41:3

I will give you back your health and heal your wounds, says the Lord.

Jeremiah 30:17a

Principle Two: Learn To Connect With Others

Isolation is one of the reasons many people remain bound. When things go wrong, some of us have a tendency to pull back from others to sort out what's going on in our minds. I call it going into hiding. The notion of withdrawing is not wrong. We all need time to resolve what's going on internally; but we were never created to completely isolate ourselves from God or from others who could help us back to restoration. If we opt to go solo, we don't benefit from the unconditional love of God and the support of those who have the ability to nurse us back to health.

Let's take the example of Jesus Christ. Jesus never remained isolated from the Father. He was in constant communion with Him, except during that time on the cross when He was carrying the sin of the world (Matthew 27:46). In addition to this, Jesus had different levels of relationships with His disciples; some were closer to Him than others. When He needed support, He called on them in His time of need (Matthew 26:36-46). He also had friends and people He hung out with. And let's not forget the crowds of people who followed Him in His ministry (Mark 15:40-41). To me, this is the perfect model that we are to adopt. We all need people close enough to us so that we can bear one another's burdens (Galatians 6:1-3, First Thessalonians 5:14). The onus is on us to find godly people to support us in getting back on track.

Looking back over the years, this model of connecting and building relationship eluded me. Though I had developed a solid relationship with God and I was surrounded by a multitude, I had not grasped the value of having a core of trusted, godly people from whom I could receive love and support or to whom I could reveal my "sorrowful and deeply distressed state" as Jesus did (Mathew 26:37-38). There were many reasons for this which I won't go into now.

To have no one around you in times when you are in great sorrow or distressed is not what God intended. When you look at God Himself, He is in relationship with Jesus, His Son and the Holy Spirit. Moreover, God Himself emphasized the importance of relationships when He created Adam and declared, *"It is not good for man to be alone. I will make a companion who will help him"* (Genesis 2:18). Though we tend to use this Scripture in reference to marriage, I believe this encompasses marriage, but refers to the larger subject matter of relationships as a whole. Just because you are single does not mean that God wants you to be alone. He has placed in your life people who can help you. Remember, help comes in many different forms.

I love the way King Solomon talked about the advantages of companionship:

> *Two people can accomplish more than twice as much as one; they get a better return for their labor. If one person falls, the other can reach out and help. But people who are alone when they fall are in real trouble. And on a cold night, two under the same blanket can gain warmth from each other. But how can one be warm*

alone? A person standing alone can be attacked and defeated, but two can stand back-to-back and conquer. Three are even better, for a triple-braided cord is not easily broken.

Ecclesiastes 4:9-12

My question to you, Sister, is this: Who is there for you in your time of need? Do you have a few trusted individuals you can pour your heart out to, who can comfort and encourage you? I have been in a place where I did not have a support mechanism and I can categorically tell you that isolation is not a place I ever want to be again!

In addition to thinking it was heinous to cry in public, I also felt there was an unspoken rule or expectation placed on those in the forefront to consistently perform and to be strong at all times. This was supposed to be the mark of a true leader. The aim was not to appear weak in front of those being led and use it as a method of building their confidence.

However, if only we all, leaders and followers alike, would keep it real, we would be more human and more approachable than the super-beings we try to be. We are human after all and frankly, I believe this notion of supposed strength is not biblically based. Didn't Jesus cry when His friend died? (John 11:35) Didn't He weep with deep sorrow just before He was arrested in Gethsemane? (Mark 14:32-42) If these are not an example of the ability to be strong and yet cry, I don't know what is.

When Jesus began to be filled with horror and deep distress, He said to Peter, James and John, *"My soul is crushed with grief to the point of death. Stay here and watch with me,"* (Mark 14:33-34). His saying this did not detract an iota from His Lordship. It simply revealed He had a human side and can understand when we are having some off moments of our own. Jesus' model of being real and relevant is one that both leaders and followers ought to follow.

Now, to balance things out, recognize that Jesus operated with extreme wisdom. Notice how all His disciples were not there with Him in the garden (Mark 14: 32). I often wonder what the reasons were. Could it be that some of them could not have handled seeing Him deeply sorrowful? Were they not mature enough to see their Saviour that way? Would it have had an impact on their faith which may have done them more harm than good? Were there some He could not trust? Whatever be the reasons, I am fully persuaded that Jesus thought it wise to simply have His trusted few around Him at such a time.

Again, I feel there is a valuable lesson here for all of us to learn, leaders and followers alike. It would be a tragedy for anyone to go through such a harrowing personal experience and yet have no one around to say, "Stay here and watch with me." I guess wisdom dictates, "Thou shalt choose carefully whom thou wouldst bring into thy inner circle." After all, aren't we all called to leadership in our own worlds? (Psalm 8:5-6)

It's now no surprise to see how the famed concept of it being lonely at the top came about. Over the past few years, my line of work has brought me into contact with a vast number of individuals of senior leadership calibre who feel this to be true. I am sure there are thousands upon thousands of others, in corporations, churches and other organizations, who feel trapped in isolation. However, it does not have to be that way! Leaders can have a support system around them of trusted individuals, from their working environment and beyond, to render support to both personal and professional matters. Part of the work I do is to provide this level of support to clients of this calibre and status so they are able to succeed in their role and create a life of lasting success enriched with purpose and balance. The benefits of having this in place are innumerable, freeing the person to excel in all that he or she does.

So gone are the days were any one of us, leader or not, should find ourselves isolated or alone. Get connected with people who can stand with you. After all, Jesus did. I don't know about you, but I'm following Jesus! His way is much better than the doctrines, traditions and ideas of men!

That little girl who had once lived and breathed God suddenly got so busy doing God's work that she even started to resent her intimate times with Him. It took away from the precious work she was doing for Him!

Principle Three: Take Time To Develop Yourself

In previous chapters, I have spent a lot of time talking about what life in the rat race looked like for me. I got so busy doing things that I left certain parts of me behind. I stopped investing in my soul. For years, I never had the time to read books, though I valued it immensely. It had been my way of feeding and developing my soul.

At one point, even prayer time became like a planned business meeting where I was the chairperson and I said what I had to say – in the allotted time, of course! I was in and out like a shot. There was no room for experiencing God's love or rest. I no longer hung around to hear His sweet voice comfort me or give me instructions for the day. That little girl who had once lived and breathed God suddenly got so busy doing God's work that she even started to resent her intimate times with Him. It took away from the precious work she was doing for Him!

I'm sure the Father must have sat there thinking, "I'll leave her to it. One day, she'll come to the end of herself and come back home." In the meantime, I was getting a serious case of burn-out.

And of course, if I was not spending quality nor quantity time with Father, there was slim chance of me having time to connect with myself each day. Gradually, I lost touch with the inner me as I focused more on the exterior aspects, such as what was going on around me.

If you don't nurture your inner being or deal with your amassing emotional baggage, you start to ingest a whole load of rubbish. Before you know it, those godly principles and teachings you held on to seem to fade away into the background, while people's opinions, fads and doctrines of men come to take the forefront of your mind. You learn to adapt to the increasing load you carry by implementing a buffer to protect you from the potentially sharp pain of the load you are carrying. In short, you become a female hybrid.

No amount of success, recognition or accomplishment is worth the high price we pay with our spirits and souls. We were never meant to sacrifice any part of our being for the sake of anything or anyone. After all, God created all parts of our beings to support each other. I don't believe any of them was meant to play second fiddle to the other. All of them need to be fed or else they will starve to death.

Anything you are doing that makes you a female hybrid is certainly not of God and it is not how He intended you to live. I don't care what role or responsibility you feel you have. The rules don't change for you because of your role or responsibility. We are all singing from the same hymn sheet, God's Word. At times, we even get carried away with our Christian duties, commitments and callings and forget to use the Word of God as a measuring stick for our lives. All that we do ought to bring about balance, peace, fulfilment, inner joy and rest to our beings. If not, I say refer to your manual, God's Word.

Remember, you are a human *being* first, not a human *doing!* This means you need to take care of your human side first before you try to do the things that you feel you should be doing. Take it from someone who has been there and has a few stories to tell. As you know, I did not start out that way; but being so preoccupied with life in itself and doing good works has a tendency to mask what is going on inside. I just thank God that He came to my rescue and I came to my senses.

Principle Four: Don't Settle Where You Are

Did you ever go through a period in your life when you got so accustomed to acting in a particular way that you eventually saw this behaviour as normal? What may have started off as something you did on an *ad hoc* basis became the norm as you got used to it.

For many it is an occasional drink, food or shopping binge that goes out of control. If you've ever been caught up in any type of addiction, you may have come to recognize that, over a period of time, these habits become a part of your life. However, just because they feel like the norm does not mean that they are right for your life. In fact, it is exactly this kind of thinking that traps you in a never-ending cycle.

The sad part is that, in our helplessness, we adapt to our new patterns of behaviour, thinking perhaps that it is our lot in life. And so, we stop fighting or looking for a solution.

So many of us get caught in this trap and then roll over and play dead, consciously or not. However, just because you have found yourself in this cycle or pattern of behaviour does not mean you ought to remain there. I know for sure, based on knowing God's Word more intimately, that this is not the life He intended for His precious daughters.

Sister, let me assure you that we can all dig deep into our mental archives and share life experiences or situations that can justify our behaviours. Lord knows many of us have been through some mind-boggling stuff, but it's still not our Father's intention for us to live as hybrid versions of the women He originally created.

Sure, things may have happened in your formative years and the woman we see today may be a reflection of that; but it is still not a reason to remain the way you are. God knew that there were going to be storms in our lives. Despite that, His desire is for us to be in a good state of health – spirit, soul and body. We only have to look into His Word and promises to remind us of how He wants so much more for us than we are attaining.

God has more in store for you — and for us all — to enjoy. So it looks like the ball is in our court.

Principle Five: Focus On Your Purpose, Not Your Agenda!

This principle was a real struggle for me, simply because I felt there were so many great things to be accomplished on planet earth. I told you how busy I was doing what I thought was God's work and sprinting through life at colossal speeds. I had joined the rat race after university. That rat race dictated that we work harder, run faster and cram even more into our already jam-packed days. This was a common theme with many high-flying corporate professionals and business owners.

It's no wonder I was working 20-hour days when I first started my own business. I had carried over the same ungodly work ethics into my new venture, all in the name of making a buck! Talk about selling your soul for a taste of success.

Many think you have to physically sign a contract with the devil for us to sell our soul in return for success, but I beg to differ. It's more subtle than that. Many may start off with all the good intentions of the world, determined to do what they believe God has asked them to do. Then they get sidetracked by other seemingly good things out there, and they justify their lack of progress with 101 reasons and Scriptures. Before they know it, they are completely off track and have deviated from what they were meant to be doing.

I have seen this happen both in the business world and the church far too often. Your life becomes packed with things God did not ask you to do. When you then add other personal and professional commitments, activities, projects, roles and responsibilities to the equation, such as parenting with its football practice, piano lessons, doctor's appointments, school meetings and so on; church commitments such as choir rehearsals, departmental meetings, prayer meetings, Bible studies, midweek services, cell group meetings or single/married couple fellowships; that's a whopping load for anyone to carry week in, week out. Then things begin to fall apart in your world. You are stressed up to your eyeballs, experiencing marital failure, broken relationships, ill health, failure in your endeavours, your children acting out and burn-out, not to mention your growing coldness toward God. By the time you get to this level, all the previous principles tend not to get a look in. And the vicious cycle continues.

Now, I am not saying that all of these activities are wrong; they aren't. However, what I am emphasizing is the impact a cluttered and busy life can have on us in the long run. It is naïve, unrealistic and even unwise to think we can cram our days to the brim, rush around on full throttle giving little or no time to resting, reflecting, recharging, reconnecting or recuperating and think it won't affect us. Not only would it affect us, it would harm us.

After running for a long time on an empty gas tank, I remember coming to the end of myself one day. I crashed to the floor of my office and a wave of emotions came over me. I was tired. I was empty. "This was not the life I bargained for," I told God.

I remember saying to myself from the onset that the Holy Spirit was going to be my business Partner and we were to take each step together. Now here I was down the line and it felt like my business Partner had gone silent on me. I now know it's more likely that I stopped listening!

My original vision was somewhat cloudy. I mentioned to a close friend of mine that I could no longer see where I was going. I did not have the foggiest idea as to when I detoured off track. All I knew is that I was no longer on the original path I felt God had set out for me. The female hybrid version of me was running the show and I was no longer in control. I was driven, all right; but I was driven by the wrong things.

Buckling under the load of what I thought were my *"good intentions and faithful deeds"* (Second Thessalonians 1:11-12), I lost track of all the times I asked God to remove the burden I was carrying. But I did not get the usual response. It was as if I were being made aware of the fact that I did have a choice, that as easy as it was for me to start doing all this stuff, it was that easy for me to let it go. I had a choice to walk away from it all and not feel condemned — even when people felt the need to add their penny's worth of counsel or start asking questions about my decisions.

God was trying to tell me that I had to let go of what was in my hands for Him to be able to place other things in my hands. I had to let go of those things I thought were as dear as life to me – especially those things that I believed I was doing for the benefit of the kingdom of God. That was hard, but I did it. I mustered all the courage I had and I let go.

And then I went on strike! I called for an industrial action on myself and refused to lift a finger without finding out what I was supposed to be doing. I can't remember how long I stopped working, but one thing was for sure: I did *nothing* until I heard that still small voice again. I was so drained at that point that I would have been happy to throw out everything I had accomplished and start all over if that was what was required. Why? Because I remembered something Jesus said about His yoke being easy and His burden being light (Matthew 11: 30). If that were truly the case, I wanted to experience it in my walk with God, in my service to Him and in my daily endeavours. It wasn't as though I had a choice in the matter; after all, I did not have an iota of energy left.

On my sabbatical, I pondered just one thing – the life of Jesus. I reflected on His simplistic, but ever-so-effective, life. You never saw Jesus running around like a headless chicken, making emotionally-based decisions, flying off the wall or living an unbalanced life. He certainly had His work/life/spirit balance sorted. He did what the Father instructed Him to do and He left the rest alone.

I'm pretty sure that Jesus could have worked flat out over His three-year ministry to ensure there was not a single sick or broken-hearted person left on earth when He died. He could have sent His mere words to heal everyone in the world, but that was not His Father's wish. And so we see the world's greatest Leader make an indelible mark on humankind for eternity in such a short period of time. I remember thinking to myself, "That's the kind of life I want."

The more I pondered it, the more I recognized that Jesus was solely focused on doing His Father's business while here on earth. Therefore, I had to take a leaf out of His book and do the same.

Was it hard dying to myself and throwing out my own agenda? Was it difficult to throw out some of the ideologies, traditions and doctrines of the people around me? Absolutely! But the more I let go of the reins of my life, the more my seemingly quiet business Partner began to speak. Much later on when I called off the industrial action, I had a renewed sense of purpose – something I would never have had while making my way through life at full speed.

In my story, the benefits of slowing down were innumerable for me as I was able to rest, deal with some longstanding issues, regain strength, refocus and get a new zest for life. Since I began doing it God's way, there has been a phenomenal difference that would require a book of its own. I am not saying it has not had its ups and downs, but I will always remain thankful for the wake-up call that brought about such a change in my entire world.

And now, this Sister's only interested in what the Father has asked me to do. All other things simply don't get a look — although I must admit, I am tempted from time to time!

JOURNALING MOMENT

The Five Principles To Living An Abundant Life

Now that you have read this chapter, I would like you to prepare a journal entry for each of the following headings:

Principle One: Get God Involved Right From The Start

Principle two: Learn To Connect With Others
Principle Three: Take Time To Develop Yourself
Principle Four: Don't Settle Where You Are
Principle Five: Focus On Your Purpose, Not Your Agenda!

For each of the principles, write down the answers to the following questions:

What was your initial response to the principle?

What has been your experience of either adhering to or straying from the principle?

How has this impacted your life?

What specific strategies and actions are you willing to implement to enhance your life?

_____

_____

_____

_____

_____

_____

_____

_____

_____

_____

_____

_____

Spend some time reflecting on your responses. To help you along the way, you may want to partner with a person or group to support you in implementing the actions you have come up with. This is particularly useful from an accountability point of view.

Have your actions, consciously or not, been telling God, "I can handle this on my own?" Have you disconnected from Him or the people He has placed in your life? Could it be that you have been so busy with life that you have neglected your very being?

Whatever your reason, why not pause to ponder it? Maybe you have been struggling with your emotional baggage and have not relinquished it to God. Or maybe you have done what I sometimes did, snatching your baggage back out of God's hands shortly after placing it there! Whatever the case, I encourage you to let go and let God control the matter 100%. You would do well to bear in mind that there is no such thing as superwomen in God's kingdom. Make no mistake, this is hard work!

The smart, godly woman who is not a female hybrid is the one God is seeking. This woman recognizes her need for God and is completely dependent on Him for every detail of her life. A smart, godly woman will recognize that it's not about being in control, but about relinquishing control to God. This is where the real power lies. Do you realize that as a daughter of God, you've been delegated power? By being an heiress to a King, you have delegated power because Daddy has all the power. So when you hand over everything to God and you get Him involved in your business, you begin to experience His awesome power.

I know this goes against the grain of some of the concepts we have picked up along the way, but it is true. We simply have to let God be God so we can stop being female hybrids and become the best versions of ourselves. This will enable all of us to start living in true fulfilment.

Chapter Twelve

Modern Traps Of Deception

*I*t's official. We have been deceived! You might be wondering how this has come to be.

One of the problems with being a female hybrid is that we accustom ourselves to the weight of our emotional baggage. Sooner or later, our emotional baggage seems to become a normal part of our daily lives. This is simply due to our constant exposure to it. It ends up muffling our sensitivity to our problems.

Think about the first time you hear a shocking story on the news, like the outbreak of war or a horrific assault. When you hear it the first time, you are moved. But as this kind of news becomes an everyday headline, as big stories tend to do these days, it loses that thing that tugged on your heartstrings the very first time. I am not saying this is good, but my point is, it isn't that the news has lost its value, but that we have come to accept this kind of news as an everyday occurrence.

Now as you know, just because something happens in a regular manner or it is a popular belief, that does not make it right. In fact, this is the basis of what I'm referring to as deceptive traps. In this section, I want to focus on the deceptive traps out there that have done one or more of the following:

- Belittle the gravity of the emotional baggage problem.
- Become widely accepted as a viable method of dealing with our emotional issues.
- Give the impression that our emotional issues have been tackled effectively.

The end result is the propagation of the emotional baggage problem.

THE MODERN EVE APPROACH

Maybe by now you have awakened to the fact that you have some emotional baggage of your own. Embarrassed, but not knowing what to do about this discovery, you endeavour to hide the evidence. You invest your efforts in cover-up techniques to deflect attention away from your baggage. Maybe you use an exuberant, outgoing personality, create the impression of success or spend copious amounts of your time, effort and money on your physical appearance. All the while, the baggage remains.

Within a short period of time, you become acclimatized to carrying around your baggage and pretending everything's OK. You simply get on with your life as best as you can. Though you may be buckling under the weight of your emotional baggage, you learn to brush that aside and get on with the job at hand. After all, you have goals to pursue, a home, business or church to run, a career ladder to climb, bills to pay, a job to do, and varying commitments. With all this going on, it's no surprise that you have little or no time to deal with your baggage. The easiest thing to do is cover up with your fig leaves.

If we take a peek behind the scenes at the Sister who has learned to cover up with an exuberant/gregarious personality or trendy/expensive clothes, we see something else entirely.

What happens when she is not in front of a crowd or when she takes off her outer apparel? When her covering comes off, she is confronted with her shortcomings and emotional issues. Not sure what to do with the shame, guilt, condemnation, helplessness and isolation she feels, she considers that the logical thing to do is to give herself a temporary fix. She might launch a food, drug, alcohol, sex or shopping binge, or do whatever it takes to give her relief, however temporary. When the occasion arises, she uses her covering aids to keep business going as usual and hide a whole load of stuff. This keeps her going till her emotions call for another fix.

This Sister sounds like a modern Eve to me. After Adam and Eve had eaten the forbidden fruit, their eyes were opened and they became aware of their true state. Confronted with their nakedness, they became ashamed. However, instead of admitting their true state to themselves and to God, they covered it up with leaves from a fig tree. The next thing they did was hide from God.

> The sad thing about the modern Eve is that she may spend the rest of her life hiding her nakedness from the very One who can heal her; unless she lets others, including God, into her world.

Sounds familiar, doesn't it? Isn't that the same thing we find ourselves doing even today? Once our eyes become open to our true state, we become ashamed and hide from God's love and the love of others who can support us in our restoration process. The sad thing about the modern Eve is that she may spend the rest of her life hiding her nakedness from the very One who can heal her; unless she lets others, including God, into her world.

This modern Eve's approach contravenes the original five principles we looked at earlier. This is the reason I emphasized the need for us to have mental and spiritual shifts. Without these shifts, if we continue to adopt notions, fads and principles outside the limit of what God has set out for us, we will be heading for a fall, just like Adam and Eve.

THE LOOK-GOOD/FEEL-GOOD NOTION

The look-good/feel-good notion shares certain aspects with the previous approach because it focuses solely on making the exterior look good with less emphasis on the interior.

This notion glorifies, over-indulges, focuses and invests in developing and nurturing particular facets of our beings, while neglecting others. Hence the lopsided adult appears amongst us.

From the past century to our present day, we have been obsessed with how we look. In the past fifty years, we have had an explosion of fads telling us what to eat, how to exercise, what to wear, what we should look like and much more.

The whole ethos of this growing obsession with our bodies is to promote the look-good/feel-good notion. This tells us that if you look good, you will feel great. While there is some element of truth in this (when you lose weight, your confidence does soar), the truth has been distorted. It is a shallow approach that looks no deeper than skin deep.

Gone are the days when the only solution to gaining weight through an unhealthy lifestyle was tackled through a regimen of healthy eating and exercise. Now, you can simply show up at a plastic surgeon who offers affordable surgery that can suck, nip or tuck you in an instant.

You have to wonder if, in the long run, this really helps solve the gluttony issue or helps those who are undisciplined. Will it help in dealing with the unmet needs that drive comfort eating and other negative behaviours? Is this really a cure for the individual who has an emptiness inside or is trying to overcome the effects of emotional baggage in her life? The answer to these is an emphatic "No!"

However, because of the heavy promotion of the look-good/feel-good notion, many people have jumped on this bandwagon and neglected the other aspects of their tripartite beings. As far as they are concerned, if they look good, they will feel great. However, we all know this is not the case. There are millions of women out there who look fantastic in our eyes, yet still have negative opinions about themselves.

How does the look-good/feel-good notion support the high-flying Sister who has not dealt with her childhood issues of sexual abuse? She may look good but still be unable to feel good on the inside until she has resolved these issues. When she finally bares her heart to someone, that person just doesn't understand why this fine Sister, who seems to have it all, can't find peace within her or experience true joy. So what does looking good really have to do with feeling good? I, for one, can certainly tell you that this shallow mentality does not work. If it did, our beautiful world would be in a better place today.

I believe instead of the look-good/feel-good notion, we should expect to feel-good/look-good – working on the inside first and letting it overflow to the outside.

If you get rid of your emotional baggage and have your personal needs met, the chances of your losing weight or even maintaining it are higher as you stop comfort eating. Simple! I believe it is high time we moved away from the message that as long as we look the part, everything will be cool. It is far from the truth. If you are totally honest with yourself, you know this not true.

We have come to discover that what lies beneath the surface is, at times, ugly. I'm sure you have seen evidence of this in your everyday life. Yet because of the look-good/feel-good notion, many never get to deal with their issues because they have, subconsciously, linked a positive outer appearance to positive inner well-being. Big mistake!

EVERYONE'S A GURU!

The wisdom of man seems to be so prevalent today. There are gurus appearing everywhere who have their own fads, philosophies and theories on every aspect of life thinkable. People will gladly internalize these notions because they are genuinely searching for answers. They want to know how to become successful leaders, perfect parents, great employees and run profitable businesses. They want to find the perfect mate, make money overnight, have the body of a god/goddess, eat junk and not gain weight, look eternally young and so much more. It seems we are looking for quick fixes, but not wanting to pay the price.

No sooner do we sign up for one fad or theory than we start looking for the next. Why? Because there is an inner void or longing that people want to satisfy. Therefore, it's no wonder many fall prey to the so-called gurus out there.

Please bear in mind that I am not saying all the stuff out there is bad. I believe God has blessed a number of people with His wisdom. The evidence can be seen in the impact it has on people's lives. My point is that many of them fail to point people to God, or they may use underlying principles that are not based on His Word, which is made of eternal truths. The result of this is that their theories, philosophies and ideas don't have a lasting impact.

Personally, I am sick and tired of seeing no change despite all of our acquired wisdom, awareness and qualifications! My frustrations have led me to prayerfully write this book with a hope that you too would stop in your tracks and prayerfully reflect on your attitudes, beliefs and behaviours.

Sister, if what you are currently doing is not working for you, I encourage you to take some time out and simply reflect on some of the untruths you may have internalized.

THE ONE-SOLUTION-FITS-ALL APPROACH

A lot of our governing bodies are guilty of doing this. A blanket approach is adopted without giving enough thought to the real needs of the people they are working for. Ineffective strategies are implemented that don't deal with root causes. The end result is that emotional issues become ongoing issues, passed down many generational lines.

So, for example, you may get governments implementing a social reform strategy to tackle the problems of teenage pregnancy or youthful delinquency. While a number of these strategies are great ideas with good intentions, I often wonder how effective they are. While they provide some establishments with the feel-good factor as they are seen to tackle real issues, many often fail in meeting their objective, which is to eradicate the problem.

Personally, I think the blanket approach simply propagates the problem. We need to be seeking out the reasons why people behave the way they do. If we were to take a closer look, we may make some profound discoveries in dealing with the issues so prevalent in our societies today, such as delinquency or teenage pregnancies. I often wonder what we would find if we were to pay more attention to what lies beneath the surface such as people's foundations (their formative years, their upbringing, etc.), and start to ask what trends are emerging. While I understand that dealing with individual cases, from a government or organization perspective, may be costly, the one-solution-fits-all approach may not yield the desired results. Also, just because a program worked elsewhere does not mean it will suit the needs of the people we are dealing with here. People are as individual as fingerprints, with differing experiences and stories to tell.

There is a lot more going on inside people than what the eye sees. While initiatives implemented have their own merits, I still think we are barely scratching the surface, as we often spend our time fire fighting or dealing with symptoms versus root causes. We have a long way to go on matters such as these and should focus our attention on probing deeper into these problems.

I also believe it is high time we bring God into the equation through the use of godly values and principles. After all, we have tried to bring about permanent change that has not yielded us the results we wanted. It is holding on to what does not work that propagates the problem for generations. The result is individuals, families, communities and nations become stuck. Therefore we remain in the never-ending cycles and are caught in a trap. This is the reason I decided to write a God-help book versus a self-help book, with a view toward achieving long-term and life-changing results.

WORKING FOR GOD VERSUS WALKING WITH GOD

Now this is a trap I personally got caught in during my early years as a young Christian. As I'd mentioned before, I was a committed Christian working for God in varying roles over the years in my church. I also had other commitments outside of church alongside my already packed schedule. And I was naïve enough to think that all that I was doing cultivated a relationship with God. I thought I was walking with God, but all I was actually achieving was doing His works. If only I had put as much passion and energy into knowing God through developing my relationship with Him as I did in serving Him, things would have been different.

Far too many of us deceive ourselves into thinking that working for God equates to walking with Him. Think about it. Does simply turning up for work each day cultivate a solid lifetime relationship with your boss? From my experience, it doesn't. All you are doing is trying to stay in their good books by meeting the objectives they set, demonstrating effective behaviours and performing well overall. Your primary reward is your pay check.

On this level, all you get to see or know about your boss is who that person is in their managerial role. However, if you wanted to build a deeper relationship with your boss as a person, it would require a whole new approach altogether. The focus would no longer be on getting your own reward, but on wanting to get to know him or her as a person. It might mean inviting your boss over for dinner in your home or meeting outside the office environment for social activities. Whichever route you took, you would have to do something extraordinary to build on that work-related relationship, right?

As you have realized, there is also a price to pay, isn't there? It will cost you in time, effort and money. Well, it is the same with God.

Simply working for Him does not build a relationship. After all, your motives for working for Him can be far and wide (guilt, recognition, selfish ambition, to gain favour). You have got to step out of your comfort zone and your realm of simply working for God to pursue Him in a way you never have before. By doing this, you move away from the Master/servant relationship and strive for the Father/daughter or even Friend/friend relationship. Now both of these take hard work, and there is a price to pay. I guess that's why many opt for the Master/servant relationship and never really get to know their God. It's easier!

Another deceptive trap many fall into is the notion that simply turning up at church services year in, year out equates to building a relationship with God. Again, I ask you to check your motives.

Some people go to church to avoid an argument on Sunday morning. I know I did at one point as a youth. Some go to look for a good spouse. Some go so they can meet up with their friends. Some go for the music, as I did before I became committed to seeking a real relationship with God. The list of reasons is endless.

You will need to pay the price by building on what is dished out to you in church on your own time. It's like having a meal on Sunday morning and then not eating again till the next Sunday morning. This would certainly have an impact on your physical being. Mere church attendance can become a ritual, especially if it is done simply to appease your conscience so you can live the way you choose from Monday to Saturday.

In earlier years, I was so carried away with working for my Father that I was not tapping into the heavenly resources that He had appropriated for me. I was not experiencing the fullness of God in the areas of my mind, will and emotions. So yes, I loved God, and I demonstrated it by working for Him; but if only I had paused to reflect every so often instead of sprinting through my godly duties, I would have realized that God did not want just my sacrifices. All He wanted was me — my heart and my love for Him. He simply wanted me, His daughter, to give Him my attention instead of focusing my attention on what I thought He wanted. He wanted me to stop running around like a headless chicken and be still in His presence to cultivate a loving relationship. I was just so fixated on getting things done for God. I tell you we have a lot to learn from the life of Jesus. After all, He came to show us a new way of walking with God compared to how the Jews in the Bible had developed their relationships with God. We need to get off the religious works mindset, as suggested in Hosea 6:6, and focus on God. I just love the way the Message Bible puts it:

> I'm after love that lasts, not more religion. I want you to know GOD, not go to more prayer meetings.

On this note, I rest my case. Selah!

C3

After you have sprinted through life for awhile with your emotional baggage firmly strapped to your back, it gets really tiring. Matters become worse when you go about trying to do things in your own strength. That's how I was with my DIY or self-help methods. And don't forget the other deceptive traps out there!

After many years of searching, my conclusion is that we simply need to enter God's rest and seek His help for our fragile state. It's all about enlisting God's help. It's not about ignoring the facts or masking your issues, but being naked yet not ashamed before God. It's all about running to His love as opposed to hiding from it. Moreover, it's not about working harder for God. It's about drawing closer to Him. Consider the words of Jesus Christ:

> *Are you tired? Worn out? Burned out on religion? Come to me. Get away with me and you'll recover your life. I'll show you how to take a real rest. Walk with me and work with me — watch how I do it. Learn the unforced rhythms of grace. I won't lay anything heavy or ill-fitting on you. Keep company with me and you'll learn to live freely and lightly.*
>
> Matthew 11:28-30, MSG

"Oh, no, that would be too easy!" I'm sure I thought when I read this in my female hybrid days. However, many years later, I got a full revelation of exactly what Jesus was referring to. By refusing God's rest, we cannot be fully restored. It's only in true rest that restoration can take place. Sister, many of us have fallen into this trap. But through the grace of God, we have been enlightened.

We have got to be mature enough as Christians to understand God's plan for our lives via an intimate relationship with Him. We should constantly have our spiritual antennae up to decipher what's really going on inside of us. To do this, we must slow down and check in with ourselves. Moreover, we have to be astute enough to recognize the various deceptive traps that have originated from ungodly principles. Jesus Christ did not go through all that trouble He went through for us to remain bound and sick. Unfortunately, many are still finding it easier to internalise the ungodly messages out there and do nothing about their plight.

ISSUES IN THE PEWS

In my personal search for emotional restoration, I remember becoming disheartened when I came to realize that an overwhelming number of Christians were carrying emotional baggage of their own. Previously, I had assumed it was simply a secular problem. Maybe it was because it was not often talked about until recent years. It did not help matters that those experiencing these problems didn't raise the alarm.

Over the years, I have come across too many Christian women who have yet to experience the freedom of living free from the emotional shackles that held them bound before they became a Christian. I found it amazing that we can experience the awesomeness of salvation, but appear to be no better off in certain parts of our lives. This was something I battled with for a long time. Why were people still trapped many years after being "saved"?

In my humble opinion, I believe once we are saved, we have a tendency to sweep a lot of things under the carpet and not bother with them as long as they don't bother us. The sad truth is that though we don't deal with the emotional baggage we hide, it still ends up bothering us. To counteract its effects, we develop female hybrid tendencies that help us mask the burdens we carry. Our masking behaviours became fashion accessories that we never fail to leave the house without.

We assume that the moment we become Christians our emotional baggage, negative experiences and a whole lot more from our pasts would simply disappear. The Bible does tell me that when we become Christians, we become a new creation:

> *What this means is that those who become Christians become new persons. They are not the same anymore, for the old life is gone. A new life has begun!*
>
> Second Corinthians 5:17

156

Though this is true, we still have to face our present realities. We still have to face the consequences of our mistakes or decisions of our pre-Christ days.

Please do not get me wrong. I am in no way belittling the work of Jesus Christ — after all, it has redeemed us from sin and eternal death. I have absolute faith in the power of God. My point here is to make you aware of the fact that there are some things you cannot simply erase.

The spiritual, physical and emotional evidence of our pre-salvation lives still exists. For example, if you had a child out of wedlock before you came to Christ, your child is still your child. He or she will not disappear and will continue to be your responsibility. If you owed a debt, had a criminal record, incurred penalties on your license or had any brushes with the law, these won't simply disappear, nor will your record be expunged or be pardoned because you are a Christian. You are still a citizen of earth and abide by earthly laws. If you were taking medication for a serious condition before you got saved, I would recommend you continue to take it and trust God for your healing. If there were negative patterns and cycles in your family such as alcoholism or divorce, it will require serious prayer to break you and your household free from these problems.

What I am saying is that just because we become Christians does not mean we can sit back and be lazy. In each and every situation, we would have to proactively seek God's help to overcome the emotional baggage we still carry. Just as in the case of salvation, you have to invite God into your situation and seek His help. Salvation is simply the beginning of our journey. Moreover, we have more parts to play, such as renewing our minds daily (Romans 12:1-2). I interpret this to mean we ought to take time out every day to proactively search, purge and cleanse our minds. I believe if we were all to implement this in our day-to-day lives, we would not be in the mess we find ourselves in today.

JOURNALING MOMENT

Practicing Sitting Still To Reflect

I would like you to pause for a second. Take time out from the treadmill you have been running on and just sit still. Lay aside all plans and thoughts for the day that might distract you. Do this for a few minutes and just be at peace within yourself.

Now I want you to ponder this chapter. Can you relate to any of these traps? Is there a chance you have fallen into one of them? If so, which one(s)? How has this affected you in terms of your behaviours, attitudes and beliefs? What steps are you now willing to take to free yourself from these traps?

Sister, this is not the time to be in denial. So be real. This is between you and God. So why not lay yourself bare before God and find your way back to His loving arms?

_____

_____

_____

_____

_____

_____

_____

_____

_____

_____

_____

_____

PART 6

Overcoming The Female Hybrid Problem

Chapter Thirteen

Revisiting The Five Principles To Living An Abundant Life

With the end for this book in sight, let me reiterate some important points before we delve into eliminating your emotional baggage once and for all.

Principle One: Get God Involved Right From The Start

Many of us fall into the trap of trying to find remedies of our own to resolve the emotional baggage we carry around with us. Often, our DIY or man-focused methods only propagate our female hybrid tendencies and create even bigger problems in our lives. Before we know it we see repeating cycles occurring, not only in our lives, but in future generations.

I believe it is high time we started to shift our focus from our abilities to God's capabilities. After all, our world today has proven that there is futility in our efforts, as King David mentioned in Psalm 60:11. Though David was speaking in the context of fighting a physical enemy, I believe we are fighting an unseen enemy that has thus far ruined many lives. David went on to say...

> *With God's help we will do mighty things, for he will trample down our foes.*
>
> Psalm 60:12

This tells me that when I get God involved in my mess, I'm sure to overcome it in His own time. No matter how educated, successful, gifted or even anointed we get, we as humans will never take God's role. Leaving God out of the equation is like being a patient who needs brain surgery and telling the surgeon you would like to be the one to perform the surgery on yourself! It's impossible! Nevertheless, we think we can operate on our souls, despite the emotional baggage we still carry. Sister, a time comes when you have to decide to place your life in the Surgeon's hands.

God knows what He is doing and works according to His own time schedule. Your job as the patient is to remain on that operating table for as long as it takes — hence the word *patient!* Imagine if you were to get up in the middle of surgery and say, "This is not working!" and storm off, or you were to keep getting up and asking the surgeon "How much longer?" Trust and faith comes into play here. When I made God my Surgeon, I no longer had to figure out how to resolve my issues. Not that I was doing a great job of this anyway! In my case, the act of merely handing over the problem to Him helped me get back to my feet, regain my balance and resume the journey He had placed before me.

Sister, this was the mind shift I had to personally make. Without enlisting the help of the greatest Surgeon, I was helpless. But by bringing Him into my situation, I embarked on my road to complete recovery. Moreover, He has already assured us of a glad welcome when we come to Him (Ephesians 3:12). After all, He sent His Son Jesus to die on the cross for us so we can be healed. So what are you waiting for?

Principle Two: Learn To Connect With Others

The benefit of external association or simply connecting with others is really to avoid the traps involved in being isolated and separated from others. For in this state we tend to spiral deeper into our despair. Man was never created to operate in isolation from God or from man. God is all about godly relationships.

I am sure you have seen the value in having godly people around to talk through things on your mind. It feels like a weight has been lifted. If you have not already done so, identify key individuals in your network who are trustworthy and loving to connect with. I suggest you have more than one so you have others to turn to if that one person is not available.

What a blessing church has been to me. Life's a hundred times richer!

Another support system you can establish is attending church. Over the years, my church became a safe haven and a home away from home. It brought together a body of people I could relate to, who spoke my lingo, shared my faith and was headed in the same direction I was. They became like family to me. We laughed together, cried together and had fun! Some of my best relationships were birthed there. Frankly speaking, I do not know how my life would have turned out had I not seen the value of this supportive community. For it was in this environment that I was able to develop my relationship with God from a young age. Attending church in a consistent fashion helped me to cultivate the lifestyle of staying connected with God. On the days I did not feel like connecting, an inspiring service nudged me gently back in the right direction. What a blessing church has been to me. Life's a hundred times richer!

JOURNALING MOMENT

What Support Systems Have You Got In Place?

Take some time to reflect on the support systems you currently have in place. Are they adequate? If not, ponder what you could do to improve your current situation. The next step is to implement your ideas.

_____

_____

_____

_____

_____

_____

_____

Principle Three: Take Time To Develop Yourself

The term "internal association" is about connecting with your own tripartite being. Just as we were not created to function in isolation from others, our tripartite beings were not created to function in isolation from each other because they need one another to function effectively.

One of the modern tragedies is that we are all so busy — too busy for relationships, too busy for God and too busy for ourselves. We just keep sprinting on the treadmills of life at colossal speeds.

There was a time I was so busy, I used to hate it when my body refused to keep up with me. Any time I felt run down or even sick, I used to get so angry with my body. Did it not understand that I had things to do? I remember in the first few years of launching out to work for myself, never having a day off sick. It was not because I was always super-duper fit, but it was simply out of the question.

Once my sister had to literally march me to bed and insist that I remain there till I felt better. I pleaded with her that I had to prepare for my monthly women's workshop, but I was told that would have to wait, since I was fighting flu symptoms. You would have thought common sense would have prevailed with me, but no. I was serving God by running programs to impact people's lives. What did common sense have to do with it?

In our busy-ness, we lead our female hybrid lives in a flurry. We all know the importance of recharging the batteries of our cellular phones so we don't experience the misfortune of having flat batteries while in the middle of nowhere. But we rarely create opportunities for ourselves to be recharged. The idea of taking time out to connect with ourselves and see what's going on with our being eludes us.

As I mentioned earlier, Jesus, the greatest Leader, made the most profound influence on earth in His short time here. He demonstrated the prime example of doing only what the Father asked Him to do and leaving the rest (John 5:19). Jesus paced Himself and was never found rushing through life – even when He heard His friend Lazarus was sick (John 11: 1-44).

Now as a reformed workaholic, I build in adequate amounts of time to check in with myself. I have cut back on running around aimlessly in order to do whatever is necessary to get me back into peak performance, connecting with God and myself.

ENLIGHTENING MOMENT

When last did you have some time out to connect with yourself? If it has been awhile, why not schedule in some time for yourself? After all, you are the sole benefactor!

Principle Four: Don't Settle Where You Are

Throughout history, we have seen God taking steps to demonstrate His desire for us to be all He created us to be. The ultimate demonstration of this desire was sending His Son, Jesus, to die for us. We now have the opportunity to live the wholesome and abundant lives God had in mind when He created us. Therefore the onus is on us to make this a reality in our lives. This means deciphering our true states – and ceasing to be female hybrids!

God is so gracious in that He sometimes brings to our attention the fact that we are living substandard lives. I just love the story of the Samaritan woman who met Jesus by the well (John 4:6-30). That was a divine appointment orchestrated by God, as Jesus did not have His disciples around to tell Him all the reasons why He should not be talking to a Samaritan woman (John 4:27). Conversely, the Samaritan woman could have come to the well with her girlfriends, who would have discouraged her from talking to a Jew. Both the disciples and her girlfriends would have ruined the chance for the life-changing encounter she would have with Jesus that day.

God knew this precious woman was no longer living the life He intended for her, and she certainly had her fair share of emotional baggage. After all, the text tells us she'd had five husbands.

Have you ever stopped to think about how she ended up with five husbands? That's a high number, even by our standards today. What was it that she was seeking from man to man? Did they abandon her or did she leave them in search of another? I wonder how people treated her after hubby number one left the scene. At a time when she probably needed their sympathy and comfort, she may have gotten judgment and condemnation instead. It's most likely people would have frowned upon her actions and called her an adulteress; a reaction that may have led her to hide her pain. If her husbands left her for other women, I could just see her heart in such a fragile state.

If she left them, some sort of emotional baggage may have lingered. Who knows how much baggage she would have been carrying around by the time she met Jesus? Unknown to her, she was a fully-fledged member of the female hybrid club. Can you believe that the female hybrid club dates right back to the Bible? Then again, the Bible does say that there is nothing new under the sun! (Ecclesiastes 1:9)

The good news was that Jesus knew all about the Samaritan woman's emotional baggage. He focused on making her realise how special she was by stating that God had a gift for her. Not only that, but He had sent the promised Messiah to share it with her. In other words, if only she saw things the way God saw them, she would abandon chasing the trivialities of life (men and water from the well) and seek the gift of God, the living water He had set aside for her. We see Jesus reinforcing her identity in God since the Jews of that time saw the Samaritans as second-class citizens.

I believe an identity crisis was part of her problem. She really didn't know who she was in God. This may have given rise to other issues such as abuse, rejection or low self-esteem. These in turn may have driven her into the arms of many men (John 4:16-18). Could it be that she was looking for intimacy, love and fulfilment in all the wrong places? It looks like she was trying to fill a void with temporary fillers when Jesus was all she needed. That's why we see how Jesus Christ enlightened her to the fact that the answer to her situation was not in the hands of mortal men. Worldly solutions offer temporary and quick fixes while with God, she could obtain an everlasting result. That's what He meant when He promised her that she would never thirst again – the perpetual spring would satisfy her eternally (verses 13-14).

To me, this story encapsulates all the principles in getting back on track to living an abundant and emotionally whole life. The story also reminds me of the love that our Father has for us and the great lengths He will go to in order to save His own children, especially in their moments of weakness. He cares for us so much that no matter what we have done or where we are in our lives, He is still willing to meet us right where we are. Isn't that consoling to know? God loves you so much that He will move mountains to reach into your situation. You might want to take a moment to meditate on that.

Principle Five: Focus On Your Purpose, Not Your Agenda!

Hopefully by now you have gotten the picture that we are all here to fulfil an assignment. Because of this, it is imperative that we put into practice the afore-mentioned principles. By doing this, we not only remain connected to God and others, we rid ourselves of emotional baggage. This now gives us room to gain an understanding and clarity as to why we are here. We are no longer driven to behaving in certain ways or forced into making decisions by any baggage we carry.

In saying this, we must also ensure we do not get carried away with our own agendas. In our day-to-day encounters with God, we ought to be consistently seeking His will for our lives so that He ordains every step we take.

Bear in mind that not every good idea is a God idea. More importantly, God may not want to channel that idea, project or initiative through you. It might be for someone else. An example of this is the way David had a desire to build God a house, but God brought this about through David's son, Solomon.

This means I too have to ensure that my ego does not get in the way. Of course, I know I can do whatever it is with my eyes closed and may be able to do it better than some others, but that is beside the point. The point is this: Does God want me to do it? So when you are about to make any major decisions or feel the urge to change jobs, professions, start a business idea or ministry, you might do well to pause and bring it before God and wait for the red, amber or green lights.

A useful mental shift I adopted was seeing God as my CEO, my Employer. Even in running my business, writing books and running programs, I take instructions from Him and answer to Him only. It took a long time for me to grasp this, as I was coming from a chaotic life of doing everything that appealed to me. Listening to my CEO meant I got timely instructions that yielded the expected results every time. I followed His vision vehemently and together we created strategies and processes to make His vision, not mine, a reality. As intelligent as we feel we are, we only see and know in part. We can't see what is round the corner unless God reveals this to us. At best, we can guess. But to have it revealed to us requires us remaining connected with Him. Living life on the go – even as a Christian — will not yield this.

ENLIGHTENING MOMENT

Scriptures To Ponder

Lead me in the right path, O LORD, or my enemies will conquer me. Tell me clearly what to do, and show me which way to turn.

Psalm 5:8

Show me the path where I should walk, O LORD; point out the right road for me to follow.

Psalm 25:4

He leads the humble in what is right, teaching them his way.

Psalm 25:9

Who are those who fear the LORD? He will show them the path they should choose.

Psalm 25:12

Friendship with the LORD is reserved for those who fear him. With them he shares the secrets of his covenant.

Psalm 25:14

The LORD says, "I will guide you along the best pathway for your life. I will advise you and watch over you. ..."

Psalm 32:8

Ask me and I will tell you some remarkable secrets about what is going to happen here.

Jeremiah 33:3

ж

ENLIGHTENING MOMENT

Sister, there is a divine purpose for your life. You did not just arrive here on planet earth nor are you a mistake. God divinely instigated you coming to this world. However, if you are to succeed in your purpose, I encourage you to make sure these principles play a key role in your life. In doing this, you avoid being a one-hit-wonder and are now in a position to create lasting success.

Chapter Fourteen

Strategies For Annihilating The Female Hybrid

ould it be that you have developed female hybrid tendencies along the way, as I did? Maybe you have been so busy with life that you have not really given it much thought up until now. Well, whatever the case, this is your opportunity to slow down and check in with yourself.

Remember I mentioned that speeding through life is one of the contributory factors as to why many women end up accumulating emotional baggage? Because we are always on the go, we don't give ourselves permission to nurture the various facets of our beings. We end up developing into lopsided adults, looking good on the outside, but not so great on the inside. This is not God's intention for our lives. He desires for us to live the abundant life in all areas of our lives. He wants us to be the original woman He created in the first place and not live as a hybrid.

When you consider the long-term impact of being a female hybrid, you will see that it influences your ability to be an effective human being. It affects your capability of carrying out your purpose, which is your mission here on earth. Living the hybrid life will eventually bring about a dysfunctional spiritual life, an inability to attain personal fulfilment, joy and lasting success – to mention a few. It also goes beyond you and starts to impinge on those who are in relationship with you, be it in the business or personal arena.

> *When you consider the long-term impact of being a female hybrid, you will see that it influences your ability to be an effective human being.*

And so, to start with, I request that you *slow down*! Take it from a former female hybrid; life is much better travelling the slow lane at a slower pace. So include copious "me time" in your schedule with the aim of pausing from the race.

To help you annihilate any female hybrid tendencies in your life, I have created a three-phase approach consisting of discovery, acceptance and action phases. Under each phase, you will find thought-provoking strategies and activities to support you in moving towards being the original woman God had in mind when He created you. They will also help you in getting on track to living the abundant life God promised us.

Now please bear in mind that Rome was not built in a day. So take your time and prayerfully read through what I share with you. Avoid the urge to skim through the activities or to bypass them altogether. I encourage you take the time to work on these as they have been created with you in mind.

172

Another suggestion I have is that as you make your way through the three phases, you may find it of value to connect with a trusted friend. Enlist him or her to talk through some of your findings or to support you regarding the actions or decisions you are about to embark on. You may also want to make yourself accountable to that person. Above all, invite God into the process.

Before we dive in, I want you to be aware of a simple fact. I am not ignorant of the fact that we are all carrying emotional baggage of varying sizes and complexity. While some may be adequately supported in getting on track to overcoming their emotional baggage through this book, others may require further professional help. If this is you, I encourage you to seek such help. I pray that Father leads you down the right path to get the godly help you require. If you do not belong to a church, you may want to pop along to your local church as your first point of call, to see what help they have to offer.

Finally, don't forget to keep the five principles to living an abundant life in the forefront of your mind. For a quick recap, I have listed them below:

> Principle One: *Get God Involved Right From The Start*
> Principle Two: *Learn To Connect With Others*
> Principle Three: *Take Time To Develop Yourself*
> Principle Four: *Don't Settle Where You Are*
> Principle Five: *Focus On Your Purpose, Not Your Agenda!*

CB

THE DISCOVERY PHASE

This phase is all about you pressing the pause button and looking inward.

UNMASKING YOUR TRUTH: GIVING YOURSELF A LIFE CHECK-UP

Sister, there is no better time than now to pause to consider your life thus far. You might find it beneficial in doing what I call a life check-up, which is a fantastic opportunity to catch up with the real you. Just the same way you go to the doctor for a physical, give your emotional life a check-up. Run some tests (below) to see how your attitudes, beliefs and behaviours are doing. Use the following check-list to prompt some thoughts:

- Have you enlisted in the female hybrid brigade? Could you relate to any of the female hybrid characteristics mentioned earlier?
- Ask yourself, "Why do I act the way I do?" And please don't answer with, "That's just how I am" or "I have always been like that". That won't wash anymore.
- Have you noticed any negative patterns or behaviours in your life of late such as addictive, compulsive or impulsive behaviours (i.e., binge eating, drinking, shopping)?
- What negative emotions have you been exhibiting lately — anger, jealousy, fear, etc.?
- Is there anything or anyone, past or present, that triggers a negative response in you such as resentment towards God or others, old habits or sins resurfacing, depression, bitterness, lack of forgiveness, lust and the like? These are signals that something is lurking beneath the surface.
- If you were to rummage through the contents of your heart, what would you find? What is the real condition of your heart?

If your attitudes, beliefs and actions are below the standards God has set for His daughters or do not line up with God's Word, you will have to decide now whether you want to remain this way or probe more deeply into why you do the things you do. As a woman of God, you simply cannot let your emotions run the show. After all, you have a mandate to follow in the footsteps of Jesus Christ every day.

Look out for anything that falls short of what you know God desires for you. To do this, you may need to get into God's Word to find out what His desires and standards are for you.

JOURNALING MOMENT

Giving Yourself A Life Check-Up

Start to prayerfully consider what is really going on in your life. Remember that the yardstick we use to measure our lives is God's Word. Therefore, answer these questions:

What fruits are you producing? Are they fruits of the Spirit or fruits of the flesh? (Refer to Galatians 5:19-26.)

If you're not producing all the fruits of the Spirit and find yourself swaying in the direction of the fruits of the flesh, why do you think this is so?

Meditate on this. Are your thoughts true, honourable, right, pure, lovely, admirable, excellent, and worthy of praise? (Refer to Philippians 4:8.)

Begin to journal what you have identified so far in your life check-up.

_____

_____

_____

_____

_____

_____

DISCOVERING WHAT LIES BENEATH: IDENTIFYING YOUR SYMPTOMS

This is where you start to look at identifying the symptoms of your issues. As mentioned before, issues are similar to physical illness in that they also display one or more symptoms. In the case of physical illness, you may experience symptoms such as pain, bleeding, swelling or increased temperature, indicating that something is not functioning well on a cellular, organic or systemic level. Doctors then use these symptoms to diagnose the source of the problem and determine which treatment will be administered.

Have you noticed that prior to doctors narrowing down the root cause of the symptoms, they tend to carry out tests? Rarely do they just treat the symptoms unless it's to provide immediate relief; even then, they are cautious. Their aim is not to misdiagnose you, as the result could be detrimental or possibly even fatal.

You can begin to draw parallels between the symptoms of issues and of physical illness in that they are both indicators of abnormalities that need to be investigated and treated accordingly. Just as doctors would not just treat the symptoms, you ought to consider doing the same too, as the consequences could be detrimental, if not deadly. Your symptoms are a cry for help, notifying you of the fact that something isn't right. Of course, you can choose to ignore or override the symptoms, but one day you will be halted in your steps and will need to seek help immediately. You know what they say: "You can run, but you can't hide!"

The truth is that the symptoms and the underlying causes of your issues will not simply disappear if you ignore them long enough. The error a number of us fall into is that we leave things to fester for a long time, which potentially causes even more problems than we started with. By doing this, even bigger problems arise.

God knew what He was doing when He instituted the concept of pain in us. It's there for a reason. If it weren't there, many lives would be cut short, as some illnesses would go undetected. It's the same with emotional issues. However, many of us just try to override the symptoms, not realizing we are doing ourselves more harm than good.

JOURNALING MOMENT

Identifying Your Symptoms

Cast your mind back to the stories of Roberta, Patricia, Tracey and Hope where we pinpointed some of the symptoms they were portraying. Notice how their attitudes, beliefs and behavioural patterns were fuelled by the life experiences and situations they had faced.

If you were to take a snapshot of your life today, what symptoms might we start to see? To help you with this, you might find it easier to write a short story of your life depicting the highs and the lows. Include behavioural patterns, attitudes, and beliefs you adopted along the way. Consider the following:

Have you been through harrowing personal circumstances? If so, what was the impact on your life? How has this affected you today?

Have you been sprinting through life at colossal speeds while neglecting certain aspects of your being? If so, what areas have you left behind and how has this affected your life?

Have you adopted some female hybrid tendencies along the way? Which tendencies are these? What do you think instigated this?

Have you been accessorising your life with the "eb" designer label, carrying your emotional issues in their various ranges of purses, hold-alls, suitcases or trunk boxes? If so, which emotional issues can you identify with? Perhaps you might revisit the list of top ten emotional baggage items women carry around with them.

Sister, use this opportunity to identify what's lying beneath your surface in the form of symptoms and behavioural patterns.

_____

_____

_____

_____

_____

_____

_____

_____

_____

_____

THE ACCEPTANCE PHASE

Now that you have made some discoveries, this phase supports you in acknowledging and accepting some truths.

ACKNOWLEDGING THE TRUTH

The first step in resolving any problem is acknowledging that a problem exists in the first place. Denying the truth only stands to prolong the matter and may have devastating results. It's like ignoring a constant pain, such as a bad headache. While the pain may be due to a whole raft of things, such as stress, lack of food or sleep or straining of the eyes, it may also be the sign of a brain tumour. Now we all know that in a number of medical conditions, the earlier you start treatment, the better the prognosis.

So what I am saying is that rather than ignore the facts, accept them for what they are and take steps to overcome them. Denial or ignorance is certainly not the way to go. Remember that we are talking about your life here. You only have one shot at it!

JOURNALING MOMENT

Embracing Your Truths

From the previous exercises, make a list in your journal of some truths about yourself that have come to light. Rather than focusing on the negatives, balance your list by including the good, the bad and the ugly.

_____

_____

_____

_____

_____

EMBRACING YOUR REALITY

By now you have had several opportunities to reflect inwardly. You may have identified some truths about your life. You may have found this easy to do, especially if your issue was staring you in the face. On the other hand, maybe you needed to do a bit of soul-searching for the subtler or less obvious issues. You may not be like the story of the woman with the issue of blood in the Bible who was constantly faced with the mess of her issues. Whether she liked it or not, she had to accept the fact that she was bleeding and deal with her loss of blood in an appropriate manner. Either way, whether your issue is glaringly obvious or not, you have to deal with whatever it is.

While in your reflective mode, look out for behaviours that you may have become accustomed to that you may brush off as being normal or acceptable. Anything below God's standard for our living is not normal, as it is unacceptable. For example, just because comfort eating has become a well-accepted way of making yourself feel better, that does not mean it is God's way of dealing with your issue; nor is retail therapy, a.k.a. buying things to make yourself feel better. As you know, these will attract more issues into your life, such as weight problems, eating disorders, health problems and debt, to mention a few.

Another thing to be aware of when reflecting inwardly is the tendency to diminish issues to make them not seem so ugly. For instance, you might have a tendency of being depressed, but you water it down by saying, "I'm just down right now." However, if what you call "being down" consistently brings thoughts of suicide, you have a bigger problem than you think. Life has a way of hitting us below the belt; but if every blow, great or small, ends up with thoughts of suicide or anything else outside of God's will for us, I think we can accurately say a serious issue exists. Maybe your issue is not depression; whatever it is, probe deeper, ask yourself what's going on and confront it.

Finally, ponder this. Which group do you fit into? Are you a member of the "frequent flyers" club, frequently flying off the handle, or the "sporadic flyers" club, periodically being tripped up by your issues? Neither reflects the image of God, by Whom you were created, and neither is God's will for your life. Both have detrimental effects and will hamper you from getting where God wants you to be. Moreover, they will prohibit you from fully enjoying all that He has prepared for you. Therefore, it matters not whether your issue is triggered every so often or plays a major part of your daily life. It still needs to be dealt with.

JOURNALING MOMENT

Embracing Who I Have Become

What we have done so far is creating the space for you to take a good look at your own reflection of the woman you have become. Next, pause and take a step back to consider the bigger picture of your life.

How has the woman you have become impacted your life as a whole?

Has it propelled you in the direction of lasting success, a meaning-ful life, personal fulfilment, internal joy, drawn you closer to God and / or others?

What impact have your issues had on those nearest and dearest to you: your peers, boss, direct reports, employees, fellow congregational members and so on?

_____

_____

_____

_____

_____

At times we get so focused on ourselves that we rarely take the time to consider the wider effects of the way we conduct our lives. So now is the time to embrace some truths about yourself.

THE ACTION PHASE

This is the phase aimed at supporting you in moving towards tak-ing action. By action, I refer to the changing of attitudes, beliefs and behaviours that contribute to your living beneath the standards God has set for you.

EMOTIONAL SPRING CLEANING: DUMPING THE CLUTTER OF YOUR LIFE

If due care is not taken to deal with our emotional baggage appro-priately, it will clutter up our lives, leaving us little room to move around and affecting our growth as a person.

The way weeds grow alongside grass on a lawn is the same way the weeds of our soul grow along with us. As we all know, if you don't treat the weeds in your garden, they eventually overrun the place, taking over the territory. Before you know it, you can't see the grass for the weeds as they spring up everywhere as if they had invited all their relatives to stay. Sooner or later, the lawn no longer resembles what the owner originally had in mind. The longer this is ignored, the worse the problem gets.

The same thing is true for luggage. If you set one piece of luggage by the door, you'll still have plenty of room to walk around it. But if you set another, then another, then another alongside it, it's going to get increasingly hard to get around it. Once you start piling the pieces on top of each other, the whole thing gets into a precarious state. They could fall at any time. As your emotional baggage piles up, it becomes a real obstacle to your life and a hazard in your daily existence. If you try to carry all this baggage with you, you are looking at a serious challenge. You'll be able to get away with carrying a few pieces, but before you know it, your baggage will be too much to carry. It will block your life and obscure you from the world. Soon it will start to influence your behaviors, attitudes and beliefs. This has been a huge contributory factor to the rise of hybrid versions of many of us. When you take a closer look at yourself, you notice that you no longer resemble the precious woman God originally had in mind. Once in this hybrid form, the quality of your life begins to deteriorate as you spend copious efforts trying to compensate for the extra weight you are carrying around. In the worst cases, female hybrids can become prisoners to their heavy baggage — crippled, blinded and bound.

Sadly, this is the state many of us find ourselves in today. The question I ask is this: Can we really run successful businesses or ministries, soar to the top of our careers, be effective leaders, wives, mothers, sisters, daughters or friends in this state? Is it at all possible to fully maximize our potentials or to embark on living purposefully in our hybrid form? Would we be in opposition to creating lasting success throughout the course of our lives? Maybe you manage to hold the fort for awhile and become a one-hit-wonder. However, there is so much more to attain in this life that God has so graciously given us. And at the end of my life, I want to able to join the ranks of people like Paul in saying:

> *I have fought a good fight, I have finished the race, and I have remained faithful. And now the prize awaits me—the crown of righteousness that the Lord, the righteous Judge, will give me on that great day of his return. ...*
>
> Second Timothy 4:7-8

I highlighted this Scripture because it ought to be our ultimate goal in life to do the very best we are capable of, especially in the area of our individual missions here on earth.

So can you now begin to see how this book goes beyond you and your emotional well-being? It's so much more than that. Personally, I find it useful to keep the end in mind. It helps me keep a check on myself.

After living through this once upon a time, I can say with my hand on my heart, that I would rather call an urgent meeting with God asking Him to beam me home than to waste a single moment travelling on life's journey carrying all that baggage around with me. Life becomes a literal pain when you travel with your emotional baggage attached to you. Sooner or later, it topples over and buries you.

Do you remember how Samson's mission was marred by his lust for women, which eventually brought about his downfall? Let's not forget King Saul's long-standing issues of an inferiority complex and low self-esteem that consumed him and drove him to commit some terrible acts.

As you start to spring clean your life, please don't leave God out of the equation. Now that you will be clearing out some unnecessary clutter, it is the perfect time to replace all that mess with God and His Word to help you change some of your attitudes and belief systems.

JOURNALING MOMENT

Dumping The Clutter Of Your Life

In dealing with your own emotional baggage, let's use an iceberg to illustrate.

Visualize a huge iceberg floating in the Antarctic. Imagine that iceberg is you. The visible parts of the iceberg, above the water line, are the things we know about you — your personality, behaviours, skills, abilities, and so on. The part below the water line that is not visible to anyone includes your beliefs systems, values, motivations, preferences, personal experiences and emotional baggage. The crucial point to bear in mind is that all the things below the water line, the things we do not get to see about you, underpin what we see — the visible part of your iceberg. In simple terms, all the areas below the water line directly influence the items above the water line.

Bearing this in mind, take a moment to consider the emotional clutter you now want to get rid of in your emotional spring cleaning.

_____

_____

_____

_____

ENLIGHTENING MOMENT

God has wonderfully and uniquely created you for such a time as this. To help you accomplish your purpose in life, He has deposited an amazing array of gifts and abilities inside you. However, with each fleeting moment that the real you fails to show up, someone somewhere misses out on a dynamic opportunity to experience God through you.

ELIMINATING ROOT CAUSES: ZAPPING THE WEEDS OF YOUR LIFE

All of us have tried pulling weeds out of our gardens, only to leave the roots in the ground. Have you noticed what happens? The weeds come back – with a vengeance! It's only a matter of time.

In my journey as a female hybrid, I repeatedly made the mistake of dealing with weeds in my garden this way. I always walked away with a smug feeling that this was my territory and I ruled things, not the weeds! However, I was fooled into believing that ripping their heads off by getting rid of what I saw on the surface had solved the problem. All I had been doing was dealing with surface issues or symptoms. I could just hear the little weeds laughing at me, saying, "So she thought she got rid of us, huh? We'll soon show her what we're made of. We may be down, but we're not out. We'll be back!"

Before you know it, the weeds rear their ugly heads again. Why? Because they have a life source, a root, that still exists in the ground. The visible parts may have been sheared off, but in the roots lie the capability to regenerate. The only way I found to effectively kill the weeds in my garden was to find something powerful enough to kill the life source, a weed killer that could reach down to the roots and eliminate them completely.

Through the behaviour of the weed, I began to understand how issues deep in our childhood could impact our lives adversely as adults. Many years ago, I heard the personal testimony of a successful businessman and minister. As an adult, Tom felt as though he had never really fit in. This was compounded by his dysfunctional family background. His father had rejected him as a boy, so he'd had little or no relationship with his father. As Tom moved from childhood to adulthood, his emotional baggage had followed him and showed up in various aspects of his life.

Somewhere along the line, Tom adopted the notion that if only he worked harder, studied harder and did even more great things, people would like him more. And so he immersed himself in many activities including gaining several advanced degrees. To escape from his past, he never sat still long enough to have to deal with his problems. Tom went on to achieve a number of accomplishments including writing books, pastoring several churches and much more, though his childhood issues were never too far from him. Unknown to the world, he had nightmares every night. After forty years, he opened up to a Christian counsellor who supported him in taking steps in dealing with his past. Tom overcame his childhood trauma and today lives a normal life – as God intended.

Tom's story embodies a number of the notions shared in this book. On the surface, everything seemed all right. The only problem was that there was so much more going on beneath the surface. There was a deficit from his childhood that had affected his development as an adult. The weeds of his younger days had continued to thrive over the years and impact Tom's beliefs, attitudes and behaviours. At one point he was convinced that the only way to gain a sense of belonging was to work harder to gain the approval of others. After all, that's what he'd had to do all his life. While this yielded what we could term success, it came at a price for himself and those around him. Had Tom not recognized his need for restoration and not done anything about it, I have no doubt he would still be in the same position he was before. He would still have accomplished a lot, but would never have known what it meant to have internal peace.

JOURNALING MOMENT

Zap The Weeds Of Your Life

Take some time to revisit the section covering the characteristics of the female hybrid. Do any of them resemble the woman you may have become?

Maybe you have been experiencing a niggling feeling deep within you. Maybe like Tom, you have nightmares or experience something out of the ordinary. Remember we said earlier that just because something has occurred for a long period of time in your life or affects a large number of people, that does not make it normal or acceptable. Rather than carry on with business as usual, consider actions you could take to overcome your situation. After all, you will need an effective weed killer to help you zap your weeds. Like Tom, you might want to consider speaking to a counsellor, especially when dealing with childhood issues or huge personal setbacks. I also suggest bringing the matter before the Lord in your quiet times.

So what weed killers will you opt for?

_____

_____

_____

_____

_____

_____

ENLIGHTENING MOMENT

Despite your mess, God will still use you for the benefit of His kingdom. However, this is not a license for you to remain the way you are. God uses everyday people like you and me to affect the lives of others. If doing this with your weeds, it's most likely that your issues will be running the show or driving you in some shape or form. This means while we are in this mode, our effectiveness is hampered if not hindered as we are in "me mode" or survival mode. Alternatively, if you are coming from a place of strength and wholeness, you will definitely be more effective and productive for God as you are no longer blinded by your needs.

REMOVING EMOTIONAL BAGGAGE: GETTING RID OF YOUR EXCESS BAGGAGE

I spent an earlier section of this book highlighting what I call the top ten examples of excess baggage women carry around with them, most of which they may either not readily admit to or not realize they are lugging around with them. Perhaps you may have accumulated some of this baggage on your journey through life. As I mentioned, it was not an exhaustive list, just the top ten I have come across. This could mean that your issue may not have been featured on the list. However, since this book is all about supporting you in living your best ever life — baggage free — I strongly encourage you not to adopt the approach that many I have come across have done, which is to continue to sprint through life acting like everything is fine when it isn't.

As you endeavour to discover the contents of your emotional baggage, I would suggest you slow down and take your time. Trying to do this on the go is not effective. Remember that some of the reasons why our emotional baggage accumulates in the first place include our pace of life and not having time to nurture ourselves. So why not carve time out of your busy schedule to work on this?

In eliminating your emotional baggage, I have shared a number of mental and spiritual shifts to enable you to change your behaviour. However, as you probably know, behaviours can take some time to change. One of the reasons is because in the case of some emotional baggage we have been carrying it since childhood. In other cases, it may have been handed down to us from past generations. What you then find is people transitioning from childhood to adulthood carrying inherited emotional baggage. Before they know it, they are repeating family history by doing the very same things their parents and grandparents and ancestors have been doing for generations.

Remember all the times you used to say as a child, "When I grow up, I will never do that" when your parents did something you didn't like? How many of us can say we were true to our word? The chances are a number of us ended up replicating the same behaviours. And so you may find yourself cooking, cleaning, spending money or even raising your children in a similar manner to your parents. Why do think this is so? Well, some other factors may have come into play:

- There has not been a strong enough change in your belief systems and mindsets to fuel a change in your behaviour.
- There hasn't been a complete willingness, a 100% commitment, to doing whatever it takes to let go of notions and behaviours of the past.
- There is an absence of new learned, corrective and effective behaviour. In trying to change your conduct, if there isn't an appropriate replacement behaviour and you don't know what to do, you will inevitably stick to what you know.
- The previous behaviours have not been unlearned to replace the old with the new. This requires a more proactive approach. For instance, imagine you had a bad habit of interrupting people so much so that it affected your ability to listen to others. While you would need to improve your listening skills, part of the learning process should include learning not to interrupt regardless of the overwhelming desire to do so.
- There are inadequate measures or support systems to support you while you endeavour to change. This could mean enlisting the help of a coach, counsellor, trusted friend, buddy, mentor or group. Your situation would determine the level of support you need. Whatever you do, try to make yourself accountable to someone. You would find this most useful especially when you are having a moment that might lead to relapsing. This concept relates to principle two that talks about connecting with others. Trust me, the benefits are innumerable.

When you are trying to eliminate what I refer to as deep-seated emotional baggage, all these behavioural shifts would need to come into play in addition to the five principles we learned about earlier on.

JOURNALING MOMENT

Getting Rid Of Your Excess Baggage

Revisit my top ten list of emotional baggage and consider which ones, if any, apply to you. If you have an emotional issue(s) that is not on the list, yet you know it exists, please make a note of it.

Describe, specifically, how the emotional issue(s) have affected your life. What impact has it had on your career, relationships, finances, well-being?

Describe what your life would be like if you could overcome the issue(s). What would an emotional baggage-free version look and feel like – both internally and externally?

What actions are you now willing to commit to in order to upgrade your life? What support mechanisms can you put in place to support you and provide accountability? Remember, your ultimate goal is to be the original woman God intended you to be. To do this, you may want to read the Bible in a consistent fashion to gain an understanding of the standards He has set for you.

_____

_____

_____

_____

_____

_____

_____

_____

_____

_____

PART 7

Pearls Of Wisdom For Your Journey To Wholeness

Chapter Fifteen

Pearls Of Wisdom From A Converted Female Hybrid

Over the course of dealing with my own emotional baggage and working alongside countless women, I have a few pearls I would like to share with you. These are essentially strategies that have helped me personally far more than I could ever have imagined. Please bear in mind that these work in unison with the original five principles for living an abundant life.

USING PRAYER AS A TOOL

I have found prayer to be the most valuable tool, not just in overcoming emotional baggage, but for excelling in all areas of my life. By cultivating a habit of having dialogues with God, I get the opportunity to pour out my heart to a Father who loves me unconditionally. In return, I get all the help I need in the form of an encouraging or loving word, direction when I need to make a decision, a healing touch and much more.

One of the things I value most about prayer is that it is my sacred time with Him and I have His full attention. I never feel like I am a burden, even though I may have raised the same problem a zillion times. I can cry as much as I want without feeling funny and He has a way of making me feel special when I leave His presence. Above all, though I may have come to Him downhearted, weighed down by some care, I always leave Him elated with His joy and peace, knowing that everything will be all right.

Sister, if you have not cultivated a lifestyle of prayer, I sincerely encourage you to start today. If there is one thing you can be sure of, it is God's desire for a relationship with you. Therefore, the onus is on you to take steps to develop a strong relationship with Him. In this day and time where there is so much going on in our lives, I cannot not fathom a life without prayer to help me soar through life. After all, there is no situation too big for Him to handle. By passing my cares to Him, I can lay my head on my pillow at night knowing fully that all will be well! Is this a peace you have? If not, get talking to God.

ENLIGHTENING MOMENT

Study The Following

Jeremiah 33:3	*Matthew 7:7-11*
Philippians 4:6-7	*First Thessalonians 5:17*
James 5:15-18	*First John 5:14-15*

DISCOVERING YOUR ROYAL HERITAGE

Everyone born into a royal family soon becomes familiar with their royal heritage. They are constantly reminded of it! The same goes for God's children. We too belong to God's royal kingdom and need to familiarize ourselves with being a child of God. This will help you in walking, talking, thinking and acting like royalty. You will also need to know the history of God's kingdom, what your ancestors got up to, rules for daily life in the kingdom, your godly rights and how to exert those rights. All this can be found in the Bible. Therefore, you will need to get familiar with its contents. How else will you get to know things like what your future inheritance will be? God has so graciously left us promises we can build our hopes on. Above all, the more you read about God, the more you will get to know Him and His ways.

Studying the Bible has another advantage in that the more you ingest of it, the more it helps you to cultivate healthy mindsets and beliefs. Sooner or later, these will filter into your behaviours. So if you have not already done so, get into the habit of reading your Bible daily. This will help you to overcome any emotional baggage you may have amassed.

SLOWING DOWN AND TAKING TIME OUT

If there is a resounding message in this book, it is the concept of decreasing the pace of your life and taking regular time out for yourself.

My utmost desire for you is to creatively find ways of reorganizing your life so you no longer have to speed through life at colossal speeds. Also, it is my hope that you will find ways of building in regular time slots in your busy schedule for some "me time" with yourself. I know some women may struggle with this as they may consider themselves having important roles, responsibilities or commitments. Or the case may be that they consider their lifestyles to be set in stone.

Regardless of your status or position, you owe it to yourself to do this. Remember a simple fact: You hold the reins of your life. In fact, God has placed you in charge of managing your life. If the way your life is going is not suited to you or beneficial to your needs, it is your responsibility to change it. So why not take time out and create new rules for your life? I have lost track of how many times I have had to do this over the years. Rather than sit there, complaining of how stressed you are or the fact that you never have time to do what you really want to do, I say you are a prime candidate for some "me time". Carve out some time and start making a list of the changes you would like to see in the differing areas of your life. The next step is finding creative ways of implementing these changes. Some changes may require a job or career change. Some may require you saying "no" more often or relinquishing some of your commitments. Whatever you do, make sure it is right for you. As usual, prayerfully consider the changes you intend to make.

If you will carve out time for yourself in a consistent fashion, you will be able to catch up with yourself. This is the forum where you get to discover things about yourself such as latent talents or emotional symptoms, reflect on them and decide what course of action to take. Your "me time" is also a time to be still, quiet, relax and rest. I find these are the best times to talk to God and hear Him clearly without everyday distractions.

Sister, you owe this to yourself. Remember one simple truth: Emotional baggage, negative emotions and behaviours and female hybrid tendencies accumulate over time because we don't slow down to invest in our beings or take the time to deal with issues.

Taking time out helps you to regain balance and perspective, neither of which you can achieve when you are sprinting through life. Many of us are caught up with the Martha syndrome. We are preoccupied with a lot of nonessential activities and neglect what is of utmost importance: our relationship with God. Rather than sit at His feet and rest in His presence, as Mary did (Luke 10:38-42), we tend to flap about like Martha and then complain that we seem to be the only one doing any work.

So the message is this: Develop the habit of taking time out for yourself regularly. In addition to this, find ways of slowing down the pace of your life.

HEALING MOMENT

Have you found yourself on the treadmills of life? Maybe you joined the rat race of life and have not stopped sprinting since then? Wherever you find yourself, why not meditate on this Scripture?

> *...Only in returning to me and waiting for me will you be saved. In quietness and confidence is your strength.*
> *...*

Isaiah 30:15

Conclusion: Embarking On Your Journey

*I*t is my sincere desire that you stop being a female hybrid and eliminate your emotional baggage, freeing you to live your best life ever.

Hopefully, you have come to realize that life is not just about succeeding externally and soaring in your career, but about prospering internally as well. It is God's desire that all aspects of your life flourish, and that includes both your spirit and your soul. He desires that we live the abundant life and experience the richness of being a daughter of God.

I pray that you will do whatever it takes for you to experience all that God has in store for you. I also pray that you will cultivate your relationship with Him more fully, so you continue to reflect His image and not that of a hybrid species.

Sister, it pays to bear in mind that life is neither a rehearsal nor a stage we perform on. It's the only opportunity we will ever get to use our God-given talents to the best of our abilities to fulfil our purpose.

Wouldn't it be a shame to let our emotional baggage or our fast-paced, hectic lives rob us of that?

If you have discovered that you have amassed emotional baggage and developed female hybrid tendencies, I encourage you to take the necessary steps to eliminate them. Don't settle for living life as a hybrid. This is not God's best for you. Moreover, the whole world is waiting for the real you to show up! The world needs what you have to offer. After all, you are an amazing woman with phenomenal potential, on a mission here on earth.

Sister, the ball in now in your court! You now have to decide whether you want to remain as you are or up your game and pursue the abundant life. Being the smart woman you are, I know you will opt for the latter. Therefore, I sincerely hope and pray that you receive all the wisdom, strength, courage and support you need as you transition to the very place God has in store for you.

Postscript: The Holy Trinity

*I*n this book I've been talking about God; but these days, it may not be safe to assume that everyone knows of God and the other members of the Holy Trinity. So permit me to introduce you to all three key Individuals you will need on your journey.

INTRODUCING GOD, MY FATHER

First, I would like to introduce you to the Creator of Heaven and Earth: God Almighty. Some of His names include "I Am," "Jehovah," "Most High God," "God of Abraham, Isaac, and Jacob".

In terms of what He means to me, He is my Father. He's my Rock, my Hiding Place in times of trouble, my Provider, my Healer and my Bodyguard. Over the years, He has made an indelible imprint on my life. He has seen me through some tough times in my life and has carried me when my feet and my faith have failed me. I would really need another twenty or so books to share with you all He has done for me so far! He's my kingly Father and I am proud to be His princess. He spoils me in more ways than any one could ever try to. He loves me unconditionally, warts 'n' all, and demonstrates grace and mercy even when I don't deserve it.

Each day He constantly reminds me of His promises and the covenant He has with me. Regardless of where I am or what I am doing, He whispers His Word to me. He imprints it on the templates of my heart. In the still of the day or night, He whispers words of hope and encouragement, the words I desperately need to keep me going (and remain sane) on this journey called life. He speaks to me through the rays of sunlight, the clouds in the sky, and all of nature. He talks to me through songs that I happen to come across just when I need them. I can't help but cry at times, because I know that I have the attention of God Almighty. I cannot escape His presence. When my heart is overwhelmed, He waters my soul and keeps me from bearing more than I can handle. When I cry, He's on hand to comfort me. When I need impromptu assistance, He is there like a shot. And just when I think I have seen every side of Him, He demonstrates His love in another way that blows me off my feet. As the Scripture says, *"Who can fathom His decisions and ways?"* (Romans 11:33-36)

Unlike me on a bad day, He remains unchanging. And for those who doubt Him, let me tell you, He is real! I only have to look at the sun, moon, stars or even my very hands typing this book to know that *Daddy is real!*

INTRODUCING JESUS

Second, I would like to introduce to you Jesus Christ. He is the Son of God Who came to earth in the form of Man, though still fully God. He came and modelled for us the lives we should live and the path we are to follow. His mission to earth ultimately involved offering His life as a sacrifice for our sins. This is why He is often referred to as the Sacrificial Lamb. His precious blood cleansed us from our sins. Without His blood, we could never be reunited with our righteous God. It is this same blood that heals us from all our sicknesses and diseases. There is healing power in the blood of the Lamb that can penetrate parts no other human or even modern science can.

No one will *ever* be able to replicate a fraction of what He accomplished for us because no one else will ever qualify as a worthy sacrifice. No one apart from Jesus Christ could pay the price to set you free from the emotional baggage you have been carrying. Above all, no one has such a powerful name, whereby at the mention of His name, sicknesses, sins and even death flee instantaneously. In fact, devils, demons, curses and the like are brought to their knees when Jesus shows up.

To me, Jesus has always been my role model, big Brother, and a Friend. He never leaves my side. And you know what? He loves me unconditionally too. Now you try getting anyone else to do that for eternity!

INTRODUCING THE HOLY SPIRIT

The final Person I want to introduce you to is the Holy Spirit, Who forms the third Person of the Holy Trinity. The moment you decide you want a relationship with God through His Son, Jesus, the Holy Spirit is available to you. He is the gift Jesus Christ promised us when He was returning to the Father (John 16:7-15). He is our gift and assurance of eternal life (Ephesians 1:13-14, Second Corinthians 5:5, Second Corinthians 1:21-22).

The Holy Spirit is also your link to God the Father, Who is also a Spirit. That's why I mentioned earlier on that we have to develop our own spirits so we can connect with God.

For me, the Holy Spirit's comforting power never ceases to amaze. When I hit rock bottom, guess Who is there to soften the blow? The Holy Spirit. He's our promised Comforter.

ॐ

Sister, in order to live the abundant life God has promised us, live a wholesome life and experience His divine healing, you have to have a relationship with Him. I have discovered that, on this journey called life, I simply cannot make it without God. I have tried life without Him and the only word that comes to my mind is "hopeless". I did not know who to turn to when life failed me. It has been through building my relationship with Him that I am who I am today. I cannot take credit for anything, even the book you are reading. And so, if you have never had a relationship with Him or you used to in the past, help is at hand. Revisit the section on spiritual shifts and take it from there.

I hope and pray that you will experience God in a way that will blow your mind and keep you in awe of Him for eternity.

About The Author

Gladys Famoriyo is an inspirational writer, international speaker and coach who has a passion to see people, especially highflying women and leaders, create a life of lasting success coupled with balance and purpose. Gladys has over a decade's experience in developing female corporate highfliers and business owners. In recent years, she has travelled nationally and internationally, developing managers and leaders both in blue chip companies and huge organizations in a vast number of industries. Gladys is also the CEO of Success Partners LTD, an international training and development corporation which provides pioneering services and products for individuals, groups and organizations. Gladys speaks to audiences worldwide with her thought-provoking, life-changing and inspiring messages.

To sign up for Gladys' inspiring eZine, eWoman, or to get information about her inspiring events, services and products, log onto www.gladysf.com.